The New Sales

Professional's Playbook

Jumpstart Your Sales Career Today

By Vincent D. Burruano

Twin Horseshoes Publishing
www.twinhorseshoes.ca
Ontario, Canada

This publication contains the opinions and ideas of its author and is designed to provide
useful information in regard to the subject matter covered. The author and publisher
are not engaged in professional services in this publication. This publication is not
intended to provide a basis for action in particular circumstances without consideration
by a competent professional. The author and publisher expressly disclaim any
responsibility for any liability, loss, or risk, personal or otherwise, which is incurred as a
consequence, directly or indirectly, of the use and application of any of the contents of
this book. While the author has made every effort to provide accurate information at
publication time, the publisher and the author assume no responsibility for author or
third-party websites or their content.

Burruano, Vincent D.
The New Sales Professionals Playbook: Jumpstart Your Sales Career Today

Includes bibliographical references.

eBook ISBN 978-1-7377703-2-9
Paperback ISBN 978-1-7377703-3-6

Nonfiction | Business & Economics | Development | Business Development
Nonfiction | Business & Economics | Sales & Selling | General
Nonfiction | Business & Economics | Mentoring & Coaching

Dedication

This book is dedicated to my friends, coworkers, and family, especially Elizabeth, Michael, Megan, and Shaylin. Thank you for all your love and support.

Table of Contents

Foreword

I have tremendous appreciation for my good friend, Vince Burruano, who gave me the opportunity to write the foreword for his latest book, *The New Sales Professional's Playbook*. This is Vince's second book on sales. His first, *A Daily Dose of Sales Wisdom*, was met with tremendous success. Where Vince's first book imparted strategic advice on how sales professionals and sales leaders can excel, Vince's latest book focuses on delivering a practical and tactical, step-by-step blueprint for unpacking and optimizing the sales process to close more business.

In this book, you will find many inspirational quotes. Vince is a big fan of sharing other people's wisdom to amplify his own and to align and solidify the lessons he teaches. If I may add my own quote to this impressive collection, "As a former collegiate athlete, I love sales. For me, it's the closest you can get to sports without having to lace up a pair of cleats." Much like the football coach he is, Vince maps out the plays that can be readily followed to hone the skills of the novice salesperson as well as the seasoned executive. You will see that Vince provides meaningful charts, graphs, and links to add new tools to your sales toolbox. Notwithstanding these valuable resources, what I find most compelling is that in addition to teaching you about how and when to use these sales tools, Vince also takes the time to explain the 'why' behind the 'how' which most books on sales tend to gloss over, if they even bother.

Vince has garnered first-hand knowledge over an impressive career in sales and sales leadership, but he is also a student of the game. As evidenced by his impressive library of books on sales, Vince continually strives to stay current on the latest trends in sales by reading books and articles that challenge his belief system, so that his approach to sales is always fresh and relevant. As a sales coach and corporate sales trainer, I can attest that this trait for continuous self-improvement is not common. In fact, it's rare...especially for a proven executive like Vince. Too many times I have worked with salespeople who were top performers on their teams but were hesitant to update their skills, staying with what worked for the last 10 or 15 years, or they were reluctant to learn how the latest technologies could be of benefit to them. As a result, their supremacy was challenged by younger and less experienced colleagues who embraced new ways of thinking about the tools they should be using and how to apply them effectively.

If you'll indulge me, here's a quick strategy for how to maximize the impact that this book will have on your sales career. Vince designed this book to be a ready resource that you can refer to on a regular basis as a reference of sales knowledge. I recommend that you focus on the "Learning Points" that Vince includes at the end of each chapter. Then, upon finishing your reading of this book, pick three learning points that most resonate with you and make a commitment to activate them at once. Next, hold yourself accountable to monitor your progress in 30 days. Check back again in 60 days and again in 90 days. By then, those learning points will have become new habits and it will be time for you to revisit Vince's book to implement three more learning points that you will make actionable. Again, hold yourself accountable to in 30, 60, and 90-day increments.

At the end of the day, selling is about building relationships to become a trusted advisor to your client and helping them make informed buying decisions. Vince is an advocate for continuous learning, and he readily admits that his should not be the only book you read regarding sales. However, if you had only one book to choose to help you improve your sales acumen and execution, you would not go wrong in selecting this one. I hope you enjoy the read.

Robert C. "Bob" Greene
CEO and Lead Sales Trainer of RCG Workgroup
https://www.linkedin.com/in/bobgreene10/

Preface

This book has been designed to assist someone new to the sales profession or someone who wants to take their career to new heights. The purpose is to provide practical advice, easy-to-understand ideas, and proven recommendations that you can quickly implement to improve your results. You will learn what I consider to be the secret to sales success. While I do not want to spoil the surprise, my overall belief is that nearly anyone who is committed to learning the art and science of selling can be successful.

The ideas and recommendations presented cover various aspects of professional selling. In addition to discussing the 'what' to do, I will explain 'how' to do it, as well as 'why' you should be engaged in these activities. The why is important because it will allow you to consider the best way to implement the new information you gain from this book and other sources. There is always more than one way to accomplish a task. What you will want to discover is the method that simultaneously brings effectiveness and efficiency together to best maximize your time and results.

In this book, you will see dialogue to represent a potential discussion between you and a prospect or client. Please recognize these scripts are being provided as an example. My recommendation to you is to rehearse the dialogue as presented so you can begin to master the language and get comfortable with the interaction. This should include role playing with your manager or another trusted sales professional so you can practice, practice, practice.

Once you have the fundamentals down, ask your partner to begin introducing new objections into the conversation. You want them to throw you some curve balls so you will experience what a prospect or client might introduce into the discussion. Don't worry if you don't have the perfect response the first time. Write down the objection and work to develop a reasonable response to each new comment until you are comfortable you can address the issue. The process of hearing and responding to various objections or comments will help you develop a well-developed response so that when you are face to face with a real prospect or client you will present a confident response. You run plays in practice so that you can execute them flawlessly on game day. The same is true in sales. Who wants to risk a potential opportunity because you failed to properly prepare for that inevitable conversation?

Often, more important than your actual response, is your ability to deliver a reasonable response in a confident manner. Remember, "55% of communication is body language, 38% is the tone of voice, and 7% is the actual words spoken."[1] How you present, rather than precisely what you say, is a significant factor in effective communication. The more interactions you have with real people, the better you will be at conducting these conversations and influencing the other person to act in a manner you desire. You want to have practiced under every

---

[1] Thompson, J. (2011, Sept. 30). *Is Nonverbal Communication a Numbers Game?: Is body language really over 90% of how we communicate?* Psychology Today. Retrieved from https://www.psychologytoday.com/ca/blog/beyond-words/201109/is-nonverbal-communication-numbers-game

conceivable situation so you will be confident when you face the situation in a real selling environment.

At the end of each chapter, I have included 'learning points' to highlight the key concepts presented. This may become a useful resource in the future when you apply the ideas presented into practice. I highly encourage you to highlight or make notes as you read this book to ensure you identify any key learning points which will help you be successful.

This book should be considered a resource that will help you jumpstart your career in sales. However, I recommend that you also consider other sources to enhance your professional development. I have yet to find one book that covers all there is to know for the sales profession. Learning should be continuous and, like any other career, the sales profession rewards those who continually develop their skills and knowledge to achieve peak performance.

Please visit my website at www.practical-sales-wisdom.com to access free content, receive updates, and ask questions. It would be my pleasure to assist you. Now, let's get started.

Vince

Section 1: Getting Started

"You don't have to be great to start, but you have to start to be great."

Zig Ziglar

Chapter 1: You're in Sales Now

Perhaps you have always wanted to pursue a career in sales because you have an entrepreneurial and competitive spirit, coupled with a strong desire to earn your worth every day. Or, perhaps, your decision to study art history in college did not generate the job opportunities you had hoped for, and you are now pursuing another option. Either way, this book can help you on your journey to success as a sales professional.

I never considered a career in sales until after I graduated college with a degree in philosophy. Originally, I pursued this course of study in hopes of attending law school. However, after graduation, I did not have the money to continue my education. While I had enjoyed studying philosophy, it did not immediately prepare me for the job market. As a matter of fact, when I first started looking for a job, in the time before the internet, I would go to the local store and purchase the newspaper to review the 'wanted' ads. Taking the papers home, I would spread them out over the kitchen table looking for an introductory position that might be a good fit. My father would pass by and ask, "Is anyone hiring any philosophers today?" I think it was his way of inspiring me to find a job. At least that is the story I have been telling myself for the last 30 years.

I would like to share my story with you before we jump into the core information. I think it will help many of you appreciate how I started in sales and offer you a perspective as we move forward. Quite frankly, there is no reason for you to have to make the same mistakes I made. Perhaps learning from my errors will allow you to develop more quickly and with fewer frustration and setbacks. And while I found personal success in sales, I am not by any means a sales guru. I was not the number one salesperson year after year in an elite global company. However, I did build a nice life for myself and my family. And, I have used what I have learned to help many other people develop a career in sales over the years. If you let me, I would be happy to help you as well.

In those early days I discovered there were quite a few opportunities for commissioned salespeople. Essentially, the company would hire and train you, but you would only get paid when you made a sale. A minimal risk proposition for the business, but a great way to enter the job market when you have limited marketable skills. I found one ad of particular interest and went to the business to apply in person. It was a job selling vacuum cleaners. These were state-of-the-art cleaning devices that sold for between $1,000 and $2,000 in the late 1980s. A significant investment even by today's standards. It was true door-to-door sales.

I only lasted about a month. I was paired with a more experienced sales professional who showed me the ropes.

After the first week, I began to question how this nice man was able to support his family. We basically went to a neighborhood and knocked on each door offering a free demonstration of the best vacuum cleaner available. You can imagine the number of times each day we encountered an "I'm not interested!", "Get lost!", or "Don't make me release the hounds!" However, it was a good experience since it provided me an insight into the world of sales. I realized, in fact, that I enjoyed selling. I liked the personal freedom to manage my time and not be stuck in an office all day. I also enjoyed meeting and speaking with different people. It reminded me a great deal of playing sports because it was competitive, and it was simple to know at the end of the day if you had won. However, I recognized very quickly that I wanted to sell to businesses and not consumers (since there was less threat of a dog attack). It was time to find a better fit for my interests and long-term aspirations. Back to the want ads.

I went to work for a few companies in the office equipment industry, selling copiers, fax machines, and similar office equipment to businesses. In these early days, most of the training I received was through reading a study guide and watching video tapes of real-life sales situations. In truth, these tapes depicted some very bad acting coupled with some not very accurate dialogue. The best training I received was when I had the opportunity to work with a seasoned sales professional who had achieved some measure of success. However, it was not really an efficient way to learn. While it was a positive experience, it was haphazard, and it never provided a true guide to know what to do, how to do it, when to do it, and why I should be doing it. It is the 'why' perspective that I hope you will find the most compelling since it will allow you to cultivate your own approach over time, since you will truly understand the reason for a particular action or recommendation.

This is again part of the art of sales. There are few hard and fast rules—it is more like a process that you need to understand and manage. The more tools you have in your toolbox, the easier it will be to have the right tool for any particular situation you may encounter. The more prepared you are, the more confident you will be, and this will assist you in demonstrating your expertise, reassuring the prospect that you are a professional capable of helping them.

This is one of the reasons I decided to write this book. Even if you have been selling for a while, you may not be entirely happy with your results. Not to worry. This book can help you as well. The information presented here is not theoretical. It has been used by me, and the many sales professionals I have trained, for nearly 30 years of selling both products and service to various businesses, government entities, and non-profit organizations in multiple metropolitan markets. My greatest joy has come from teaching and coaching new sales professionals to help them realize their full potential. Now, I get to share this Practical Sales Wisdom™ with you.

Often, we struggle to build a stable structure, not due to lack of skill, but because we failed to spend sufficient time preparing a solid foundation upon which to build the structure. This book is going to help you build a sturdy foundation upon which you can build a successful career as a high-performing sales professional. It is not designed to be a theoretical treatise but a practical guidebook of skills and techniques that you can start using to improve your performance today. My hope is that you read the book and then use it as a reference as you implement the ideas and suggestions presented. Remember, it is in the execution that you will realize the benefits of this information.

Initially, I looked at sales as just a job. It was not until I started to think about it as a career that my mindset evolved. In the beginning, I would arrive at work on time and go through the motions until it was time to leave. I did what I was told, making phone calls or cold calling in my territory. I was good at following directions, but my ambition and enthusiasm were not at a level that would allow me to be highly successful. I had not fully embraced the idea of sales as a profession where I could determine what I was paid based on my performance. Most jobs pay you a salary and you may get a small merit increase each year if you do good work. In sales, you can give yourself a raise anytime you feel you deserve it just by going out and making another sale. You get to determine how much money you really want to earn and can take the steps necessary to achieve your goal. Few careers offer this opportunity. While having a college or advanced degree can be helpful, it is certainly not a requirement for success. It is really empowering when you think about it, and it changed my life.

In the beginning I was making less than most of my friends. Let's face it, I was broke, and had few good prospects for improving my situation. While I had earned a college degree, what I studied did not provide me with a specific skill set which was immediately marketable. But a little initial success brought forth a whole new mindset for me. I remember generating my first few sales and receiving the commission checks. It got me thinking in a whole new direction. Once I determined that selling was no longer just a job, but my calling, I quickly accelerated my efforts and surpassed most of what my friends were earning. More importantly, I was happy with my career choice. It provided me great freedom and flexibility to live my life the way I wanted. I could work more today to free up time tomorrow, to play golf or meet with friends. I was not being judged by my activities or being in the office for eight hours each day, but by my results. Sales. Yes, being in sales means your results are easily measured and known to all. You are either making sales or you are not. You are either generating revenue for the company or you are not. You are either delivering results or you are not. It is the simplest of all score cards. Period. And we all know when you are making sales, and exceeding your goals, a smart manager will give you greater latitude to plan your work and manage your time the way you desire. What other professions offer this flexibility? Not many.

I have often described sales as owning a franchise. While you are working for a company, you are also building your own business like someone who operates a franchise. While the company is the umbrella organization which you represent, you will also be representing and building your personal brand. You a part of the greater organization, but offer a unique twist based on your personal style and approach. It can also provide you the opportunity to embrace an entrepreneurial mindset. The best organizations to work for will be those which will inspire and fuel this thought process. This way you can achieve the level of success and income you desire. You are in control. You are driving the results. People must buy you as much as they buy your company and your products or services.[2] You are one of the key differentiating factors in the process. Be sure to leverage every advantage you can to improve your opportunity for success.

Further, "only 23% of buyers agree that sellers 'always' put the buyer first."[3] Today, more than ever, being a sales professional is not simply being proficient at persuasion, it is about being a businessperson who can help clients solve problems.[4] The best sales professionals have a client mindset. These high performers are constantly thinking how they can help other people achieve their goals and objectives to meet the rising expectations buyers have.

[2] Blount, J. (2010, June 21). *People Buy You: The Real Secret to What Matters Most in Business*. Wiley.

[3] Lister, J. (2021, July 8). *The LinkedIn State of Sales Report 2021*. LinkedIn. Retrieved March 14, 2022 from https://www.linkedin.com/business/sales/blog/trends/the-linkedin-state-of-sales-report-2021

[4] Rackham, N. (2016, May 20). *Five Mega-Trends That Have Redefined Selling*. Institute for Excellence in Sales. https://i4esbd.com/event/neilrackham-ies052016/

Being focused on your client is the best way to demonstrate your interest in helping them realize success which will lead to your success as well.

Learning Points:

1. Sales is a set of skills that anyone can learn and develop to be successful. You must decide if you are willing to put forth the time and effort to be a sales professional.

2. Learn the 'why' behind specific actions or activities. Understand at a deeper level the art, so you can fine-tune and personalize your approach to continuously improve.

3. Sales results are what matter most. There is a simple scorecard, have you generated business for you and your company or not? You will know where you stand based on the results you create versus the expectations that have been established.

4. You determine your worth and earning potential. Your efforts directly correlate to earning the income you

want to enjoy the lifestyle you desire. While you are employed by a company you also work for yourself.

"Accept the challenges so you can feel the exhilaration of victory."

George S. Patton Jr.

"Poverty is when large efforts produce small results.

Wealth is when small efforts produce large results."

David George

Chapter 2: The Secret to Sales Success

In this chapter I will share with you the secret to sales success. It is the one thing you need to know in order to ensure your future success in the profession of sales. Most, if not all, salespeople have been pursuing this kernel of knowledge just as archeologists have scoured ancient ruins in search of the Holy Grail.[5] But in the next few paragraphs, I am going to share this information with you.

You see, the sales profession is a craft. It is a combination of both art and science. The best way to explain this concept is to compare it to cooking. Let us suppose you wanted to make a big pot of chili for a party, but you have never made chili before. You would be right to reference a

[5] Merriam-Webster. (n.d.). *Holy Grail*. Retrieved Feb. 1, 2022, from https://www.merriam-webster.com/dictionary/Holy%20Grail

recipe or cookbook for guidance. You would follow the specific directions, the 'science' of making chili. However, you would soon learn there are different ways to mix and match the various ingredients to prepare a variety of chilis. The options are almost endless, and each tasty mixture is a result of your own creativity. This part is the 'art' of chili making.

Like cooking, there is the science which establishes the fundamental rules or guidelines for professional selling and then there is the artistic part that allows you to add your own style and creativity. The important thing to understand is that if you fail to honor the scientific parts, the artistic part may be compromised, and the overall effort will likely fail. For example, if you do not properly cook the meat before adding in the other ingredients, you might find that the chili doesn't taste very good, or it might even make you ill. Therefore, it is important to understand the balance between the science and art of any craft.

Now it is time for me to reveal the secret to professional selling. Are you ready? Here it is, in a nutshell: there is no secret to success in selling. Got it? Let me repeat it just to be sure: there is no secret to success in selling. Oh, look at the expression upon your face?!? You look disappointed. To be honest, upon discovering this secret, I was as well. This is also the case for the many people I have shared this secret with over the years. Before you get angry, and toss this book aside, please give me a chance to explain.

When I was first in sales, I wanted to know why some people were so successful and others just came and floundered along the way. It seemed logical that there must be some "secret sauce" which allowed a select group of salespeople to flourish while the rest lived paycheck to paycheck. These highly-successful sales professionals must know something, or be doing something, radically different to explain the significant difference in results. It was not simply that the top performers were selling 10% more or earning 20% more. No, they were selling and earning a multiple – sometimes two, three, or even more – times every month. They were selling machines earning top dollar. And, most importantly, they were happy!

Then I figured it out. Lightning struck. I had an epiphany. The difference between the highly-successful sales professionals and everyone else became crystal clear in my mind. The high performers did the things the others simply refused to do. It was just that simple. No, it was not because their sales managers liked them better or they had been assigned a better territory. It was because they were committed to doing the things the other salespeople saw as 'hard work' and either did not do them well or simply refused to do them at all.

You see, there has been so much written on the profession of sales that there are, in my opinion, no secrets. Occasionally someone boasts to having a secret way to achieve sales success, but I think you will find beyond the occasional 'super pundit' general agreement, if there is anything you want to know about selling it is readily available. And while there may be different approaches based on what you are selling, and to whom, there is still plenty of information available for your consideration. Beyond this book, you could find many more that can help you become better at any number of critical selling skills – from prospecting, to writing better recommendations, to handling objections and negotiating contracts. There are literally a plethora of fantastic books, videos, and podcasts available on every aspect of selling. And I certainly encourage you to take advantage of the opportunity to learn more about our profession each day. I occasionally point out some of my favorites throughout the book as well as providing a complete listing in the Recommended Reading section at the end.

Only a select few become high performers in our profession despite the wealth of information available. There is a select group who become the elite sales professional or ultra-high performers. Why? The answer is quite simple. The top 10% are willing to do what the rest are unwilling to do. Notice I did not say they know something the rest do not. Though this may be the case initially, as we have already discussed, the amount of information readily available does not prevent this knowledge from being obtained by anyone and everyone. No, it is not the lack of knowledge, but the unwillingness to apply this knowledge, best practices, and techniques, which is the key differentiator between mediocrity and success. The very best sales professionals are willing to learn their craft, continuously develop their skills, create value for their clients, and then invest their time in the doing the right activities, properly, and consistently. This is what sets the high-performing sales professionals apart from the rest.

There you have it. The secret to success in sales. Unfortunately, most people want a short cut. I have seen this time and again as a sales leader. If I tell my team it takes five steps to close a deal, they want to do it in four steps. If I tell someone it will take 15 minutes to properly prepare for a sales call using the checklist provided, they want to do it in 10 minutes without the checklist. There is this burning desire to do everything faster and still achieve the same results. I am not opposed to the enthusiasm for discovering a more efficient way to proceed, but when you substitute efficiency for effectiveness, you will generally be disappointed with the results. Effectiveness is what matters most. Yes, you need to be efficient at doing the right things correctly but doing the wrong things quickly will not make a tasty pot of chili.

Don't be concerned that there is no real secret to success in sales. You see, even though the information to be successful is readily available, about 90% of the people in our profession will not seek it out or use it consistently. They will not read the many wonderful books written that could help them become more effective. Nor will they avail themselves of the podcasts that share best practices and could quickly help them improve their performance. No, they are quite satisfied with what they are doing already. Because, for some reason, it is just too hard to do it the right way. They will continue to do what they do because they believe it is in their best interest despite their lackluster results. They will justify their mediocre performance based on any number of factors, including their sales territory, the lack of qualified buyers, the local economy, prices that are too high, and even the competition. They will bark at the moon and howl long into the night to avoid facing the truth. And the truth is very simple. They will never acknowledge the one thing they can impact – themselves – as the real reason for their current level of mediocrity.

To a certain degree, there will be people who purchase this book, read it, and then keep on doing what they have always done. Quite frankly, it is a shame. I encourage you not to be one of those people. Someone so close to taking their career to the next level only to fall back in the rut. The difference between being a salesperson and an ultra-high-performing sales professional is in so many little things almost anyone can learn to do. Take the opportunity to embrace change for the better. Take charge of your own success starting now.

This is one of the great ironies of the sales profession. Anyone who wants to join our profession, who is willing to put forth the time and effort, can be successful. You must be willing to learn the fundamentals and execute. And like any other profession, you must be committed to continuous improvement and development. There is nothing complicated here. You do not need an advanced degree, or 20 years of experience. While those things may help you, there is absolutely no reason you cannot start being successful in your sales career today.

You will find ultra-high performers across all industries as well. You can find well-compensated and successful sales professionals selling SaaS, moving services, building materials, landscaping services, medical devices, and office equipment. It is truly a profession that rewards results despite the specific industry, product, or service being sold. It also provides you with tremendous mobility. What organization in any part of the country would not welcome the opportunity to add a high-performing sales professional to their team? Think of the flexibility you will have to live the life you want without limitations or restrictions. It is truly a wonderful opportunity if you decide to pursue it to the fullest.

The purpose of this book is to outline some of the best practices, when done correctly and consistently, that can lead to improved results. Please do not confuse this with perfect results. I cannot promise you perfection. However, as Vince Lombardi once said, "Gentleman, we will chase perfection, and we will chase it relentlessly, knowing all the while we can never attain it. But along the way, we shall catch excellence." I would like you to think about your journey in those terms. Anyone who promises you perfection, or a magic formula to instant success, is probably not telling you the whole truth.

Learning Points:

1. There is no secret to sales success. You simply must be willing to consistently do the right things correctly. Do what the 90% of other salespeople refuse to do and become a higher-performance sales professional.

2. This book is a starting point. Take what has been provided and put it to immediate use. Then, review the Recommended Reading section at the end of this book and be sure to incorporate learning and professional development as a daily routine. Commit to continuous

improvement every day and you will find that you continue to get better every day.

3. Becoming a high-performing sales professional will offer you tremendous opportunities to work where you want, how you want, when you want. Take advantage of this unique proposition to build the life you desire.

"Don't make 'hope' your business plan. It's not enough to want it. You have to work it!"

Mary Christensen

"Motivation is what gets you started. Habit is what keeps you going."

Jim Ryun

Chapter 3: Organized for Success

It is important to spend time organizing yourself for success. This section is going to cover several topics to help you be prepared to do your best work and to demonstrate your professionalism. A few of the items may seem obvious, even mundane, but please do not leave anything to chance. Sales is a daily challenge, requiring grit, and if you can tip the scale in your favor, even just a little, you will position yourself to take advantage of every opportunity. In sales there is never just one important thing which will make the difference, but a collection of small things that lead to success.

Technology and CRM

Most companies will provide you with the technology (laptop and software) that you need to do your work. If they do not, consider investing in your own equipment to maximize your productivity. Be sure that you fully understand how to use the various systems that will require your attention. This is especially true with the CRM system. This software tool is used to organize territories and provide you a way to manage all the information. It is common for companies to use this to track and manage your activities. This might include entering sales meetings, new opportunities, your pipeline, and your monthly and quarterly forecast to name a few. Yes, you have a boss, and they need to know what you are doing. The easier you make it for them to see what you are doing, the less likely they are to bother you for updates. Active engagement breeds a certain amount of trust and freedom.

However, I can tell you for certain that a good CRM tool will also assist you in your quest to be successful in sales. You need to understand how to use it to your advantage. Go back and read that sentence again. You must learn how to leverage the tool to provide you benefits and not simply be a method for tracking activities for management's purposes. I can assure you that every tool offers sales professionals benefits. It is simply a matter of learning what those benefits are and to ensure that you know how to best utilize the tool to realize those benefits. Outside of the data the company wants to collect, how is the tool able to capture the information that will allow you to best organize your efforts for maximum results. This would include all the contact information including names, titles, locations, as well as phone and email addresses. This should be a repository for any piece of important information you may need to access even if you decide to maintain hard copy records or files.

You should determine the 'triggers' for your business and ensure that you carefully track this information. A trigger is an event which will likely require whatever you are selling. For example, if you are working with companies that generally buy what you sell when they move, you will want to track the lease expiration date for their office or other facilities (month and year) so you can engage them far enough in advance. Perhaps you sell a type of equipment that has a general life span of about five years, you will want to know when your prospect acquired their current unit so you can know when it makes sense to call on them in the future. Again, knowing this will help you gauge the best time to follow up. In any event, these dates are trigger points for when the prospect will likely need to take some action. Every business or industry will have a different trigger point. Learn what trigger point is applicable for your business and track it relentlessly. Depending on the typical sales cycle, and your ability to promote an early decision, you will want to work backwards in time to ensure you engage the prospect early enough to be a consideration and influence the outcome.

This will also allow you to promote continuity from meeting-to-meeting building upon your last conversation to move the opportunity forward. You should also be able to note the next time you are supposed to contact that person whether it is in a few days or in several months. Even if you have a limited number of companies in your territory, do not count on your excellent memory to recall every detail. Enter the information, next steps, and to-do items in the system. Allow the tool to keep track of the mundane so you can stay focused on the strategic nature of sales.

For example, when you visit a client, is there an easy way to record some notes afterwards about your visit. This should include key topics discussed as well as to follow up on any commitments or tasks which will require your attention. Maintaining good notes is a great way to show your prospects and clients you respect their time and can be counted on to address follow up items as promised. This leads to the development of trust. Trust is simply doing what you say you are going to do when you say you will do it. When this occurs, your prospect will see you are trustworthy leading the way to a better relationship.

Workspaces

You may be assigned a workspace at your company or perhaps you will work remotely. Either way, you should set yourself up for success by ensuring you have a quiet and well-organized area to work. Even if you will primarily work in the office, you should establish an area at home to be a workspace. Be sure you have everything you need available to work efficiently. Even the little things, like a good stapler, pens, and notepads should be easily accessible in all your workspaces. You should also keep copies of any printed material you may want to provide at a meeting as well as have access to a high-quality printer/copier/scanner for letters, recommendations, and contracts.

If the work environment is not particularly quiet, think about a shared space you can use to make phone or video calls to ensure you are not interrupted or your prospect is not distracted by background noise. Consider obtaining a headset with a microphone that will allow you to appear to be in a more secluded setting when making proactive outbound calls or answering inquiries. If you use video to make sales calls, ensure the area directly behind you is a protected space. You should make sure there is no foot traffic or other potential distractions your prospect may see during the video meeting. Yes, this is a little thing until the prospect asks you if you are sitting at a bus stop in Times

Square because your coworkers are engaging in a game of "who can be the most obnoxious" right behind you. Again, ensure your workspace demonstrates your commitment to professionalism.

And do not forget your car. Again, if you are an outside sales professional who visits clients in person, you will experience windshield time and need to have everything you might need with you as well. It is a good idea to purchase an organizer you can keep in your car with extra supplies, samples, brochures, token gifts, and anything else you may need when you are out for the day visiting people. Remember, you do not want to waste time running back to the office because you forgot something. Have everything at the ready. As the Scouts say, "be prepared!"

Field Offices

In addition to your main office, home office, and mobile office (car), if you are spending time in your territory you may want to identify some suitable 'field' offices. While coffee shops can often be a comfortable place to recharge and get connected, there are other places which offer similar accommodations. Consider a large or prestigious hotel, for example. You can go in and set up in the lounge, or in the courtyard on a beautiful day, order a beverage, and connect with probably less noise and distractions than your typical coffee shop. This is especially relevant if you plan to make some proactive calls while catching up on email. Generally, hotels are happy to have people in their lounge working since it conveys a professional image to their guests.

Developing An Annual Business Plan

While many organizations will require you to develop an annual business plan, even if they do not, you should create one for yourself. I have always required it of the sales team I have led, and I have made it a point to tell them this is for you, it is not for me. In the beginning, I would get some puzzled stares. What do you mean it is for me? You told me to do it. Yes, I asked you to complete it, but it is a document for your benefit. An annual business plan is a great way to get a high-level overview of your assignment and potential for the coming year. More importantly, it is a tool to have a very honest conversation with yourself. To initiate that conversation, you want to ask yourself this question, "Do I know how I can maximize my results and earnings in the coming year?" Simple but powerful.

If you do not take the time to plan your efforts, you will find yourself all over the map. You will end up being reactive rather than proactive. As with anything else, it is better to be thoughtful about the direction and plan out some mile markers to evaluate your progress. No journey can be perfectly designed, but you can determine your direction and destination by establishing some milestones along the way. I have included an example of a business plan you can access online at www.practical-sales-wisdom.com.

While developing the plan is the first step, it is not the final step. It is essential that you consider this plan a living document. You should schedule to conduct periodic reviews to evaluate your progress on either a monthly or quarterly basis. It is a great way to manage your progress and fine-tune your approach. If you identified specific accounts to target, have an honest conversation about your progress. If some things are working better than others, make a note. If you have yet to make progress on a stated goal or objective, evaluate if it is still applicable and take the appropriate action. The other advantage of this process is the ability to roll the plan for this year into your plan for next year with ongoing updates. Instead of starting from scratch each year, your business plans will seamlessly stream together from year to year.

Again, the business plan should be a tool to plan your strategic direction as well as prompt you to have an honest conversation with yourself. For example, if you originally set a goal to generate $200,000 in the first quarter, and your first quarter results are only $100,000, you should ask yourself why. The same if you achieve results of $300,000. What did you do specifically that aided you in achieving that level of performance? If you are under plan, what contributed to the shortfall? If you are over plan, can you identify the deals that contributed to your success, and, more importantly, the activities that led up to you having the opportunity in the first place?

This is an opportunity to hold yourself accountable. Focus on what you did, or did not do, to achieve your result. Avoid blaming anything outside your control. This is a time for brutal honesty. Focus on what is in your span of control since this is the area in which you can take action to improve or generate further momentum to overachieve. Good questions include, "Will I be able to keep this pace for the balance of the year?" and "Was my win rate greater than initially expected?" and "Do I have a sufficient pipeline to continue this pace?"

Yes, your sales manager could stand over you and demand answers to these questions. However, it is far more important for you to hold yourself accountable for your own performance. You should want to understand what is contributing to your level of success. If it is a matter of luck, so be it. But people often make their own luck by doing all the little things to give themselves the best chance to capitalize on each opportunity. Whether you are behind or ahead, take the time to think through what is working, so you can do more of it, and what is not working, so you can minimize those activities. Continual evaluation of your progress and results will help you fine-tune your approach and achieve even greater results over time.

Your business plan should include:

- Sales Activities – Goals
- Account Management – Current Client Expansion Business Opportunities
- Top 5 Net New Business Accounts & Strategy
- Association & Networking Participation
- Pipeline & Opportunity Management
- Business Development Activities
- Professional Development

Managing Your Manager

Everyone has a manager or boss. Today, it is even more important to select the right supervisor than it is to select the right company to work. Your relationship with your immediate manager will be one of the key differentiators in your development, your success, and your happiness. This is especially true you are new to the sales profession. Having the right manager or, as I prefer, leader is essential.

You want someone who is capable and interested in your long-term personal development and success. I was fortunate to have worked for several great leaders early in my career who took in an interest in me as a person and not just someone who was just on their sales team. It made a difference in my ability to learn the business and to receive the support I needed to grow. Further, they were able to help me secure some initial success to feel a sense of accomplishment and remain focused to getting a little better each day. This is especially important when you are just starting as a sales professional. Their guidance also paved the way for me to receive promotions to higher-level sales positions and eventually to sales management. Their assistance and support made all the difference in my success.

 Visit www.practical-sales-wisdom.com to access the **Expectations for Success Planner**.

You can go and work for a fantastic company with a great reputation, but if you are assigned to a sub-par manager you may find yourself regretting your choice. There is an adage that people do not quit companies, they quit their immediate supervisor. I believe this to be true. I highly encourage you to interview your potential future manager as much as you are interviewed by them, when applying for a position or evaluating a new role inside your current organization. You may want to ask to speak to one or two people on their team to get an inside perspective of what it is like to work for this person. What is their reputation as a sales leader? How do they respond to requests for assistance? Are they upbeat and positive or moody? Do they have your back when there is a challenge or just go by "the book"? You will certainly learn a great deal from the responses received about the character of the person. You will also learn what effort they put forth in both your personal and professional development.

While this person is by function responsible for managing you, please keep in mind you should also manage them, or, more importantly, the relationship you will develop together. I can tell you from experience that being a sales leader is challenging. The sales professionals I enjoy working with the most were not always the ones who generated the most revenue. The strongest relationships were formed between the ones that worked to support me as much as I supported them. It was a symbiotic relationship which motivated me to ensure I was doing everything I could to take a personal interest in their success and development. In return, I could count on them to perform at a high level and jump in to assist me when needed. Yes, developing them was part of my job responsibilities, but when you are managing a large team, you have limited time available. You make choices where to invest your time just like anyone else. You want to be the type of sales professional your manager wants to spend time with and assist as much as possible. You want a mutually-beneficial relationship with your sales manager.

So, what is the best way to do this? Well, for starters, generate revenue. Making sales and being a productive member of the team is certainly a great starting point. However, it is a little bit more complicated since generating revenue is not the only criteria for building a great relationship. You need to uncover what other things are important to your sales manager, especially those little things to make their life easier. It might be as simple of submitting a weekly report every Monday morning. Yes, you do not enjoy doing this, but your manager needs the information for a report they must submit to their manager. And chances are, they are not thrilled with this task either. But in doing these small tasks, on time, without prompts or reminders, you will demonstrate your commitment to being a good team member. And, more importantly, you will make their job easier. Yes, it is a little thing, but as we will see, the little things add up to make a big difference. Or perhaps it is submitting your expense report on time or similar administrative tasks like submitting a complete order package to the client success team for processing. Whatever these things are, and as trivial as they appear, understand your manager has a manager (boss) as well, and your manager always wants to demonstrate their competency by having all their work done correctly and submitted on time.

Your work is a reflection on them as much as it is a reflection on you. You want to help them be a shining example of what it means to be a good sales leader. The more you can contribute to that success the better. You will find over time when given the choice to spend time helping you, or someone else, you receive the extra attention you need first. No, this may not be fair, but life is not designed to be fair. Life is life. Understand how people think and are motivated to behave so you can establish mutually-beneficial relationships with people.

Learning Points:

1. You should set yourself up for success by ensuring you have proper places to do your best work. Do not leave this to chance. Preparation is the key to productivity.

2. Ensure that you use your car for more than transportation. It is a mobile office and should be properly stocked with everything you might need during the work week. Keep things organized and easily accessible so you can maximize your selling time and avoid unnecessary trips to the office. You can also learn

on the go by listening to audio books or podcasts to keep your mind sharp.

3. Trust is critical. It is nothing more than demonstrating your ability to keep promises. So, when you make a commitment to anyone make sure you do what you say you will do in the period you committed. Trust is difficult to develop but easy to lose. It is also the foundation of all meaningful relationships, both personal and professional.

4. Your annual business plan should be a tool to set strategic direction for the upcoming year. You should schedule regular appointments with yourself to review the plan and compare your plan to your results. What is working? What needs improvement? How can I do even better? A business plan is a living document. Invest time on a regular basis to assess your progress and fine-tune your approach.

5. Learn to manage your manager. Understand what little things you can do to develop a strong relationship by completing all tasks correctly and on time, in addition

to generating consistent revenue. Develop a mutually-beneficial relationship with your manager so they will be eager to help and develop you.

"Most people think 'selling' is the same as 'talking.' But the most effective salespeople know that listening is the most important part of their job."

Roy Bartell

"Remember, you only have to succeed the last time."
Brian Tracy

Chapter 4: Territory Management and Target Accounts

Each company will have a different approach to establishing sales territories. Sometime the assignments are based on geography from a single town to a large portion of the country. Other companies may use an account territory list which identifies specific companies you will be responsible to manage. Often these lists cover a wide geographic area or are based on specific industries or vertical markets. In either of these cases your account list is generally your protected territory assignment. Ideally, only you should be calling on these companies. However, there are some companies, because of their specific industry, which do not have assigned or protected territory assignments. Rather, they have assigned relationships where you can pursue business in an overlapping fashion with your coworkers.

No matter what strategy your company uses to denote territory assignments, you should be certain to understand the boundaries of your assignment and what rules govern pursuing an opportunity outside your defined territory. You want to be sure the time you invest with any prospect is going to pay dividends for you. I have experienced some interesting situations when it comes to sales territories. For example, I once called on a point of contact in a company with multiple locations. One location was in my territory while the second location was in another assigned territory. I was working to sell this company a particular solution. They finally decided to purchase it, but they determined it would be best to install the solution in their other office which was outside my territory. The sale went through, but given our rules of engagement, I did not earn sales credit or a commission on the transaction. Important lesson learned.

Whatever method your company uses is less important than what you do once you have your assignment. At that point, it is time to conduct an analysis of your territory so you can begin to develop a business plan for how you will engage clients, identify prospects, and generate new opportunities. You can do this even as you are learning the technical aspects of selling the products and services your company offers. It will take extensive research and time to complete this task initially. However, please understand you will make this a normal part of your territory management process. Things evolve and change so you will need to stay current with your research and territory analysis.

You should start with learning about your company's best clients. Even if you will not be assigned to work with these firms, you should take the time to learn about them. In this way you will be able to construct an Ideal Client Profile (ICP). This is a great tool to help you identify the characteristics of your preferred client. And it is learning about existing clients that will help you develop a prospect list with similar looking companies to pursue. The act of defining those unique characteristics will let you research and investigate other firms with similar attributes. This is a great way to start identifying your target list. Remember, we segment markets to find how we can create differentiation in each key market for specific prospects.[6] Segmenting also allows you to understand the unique pains and gains for each industry and then to incorporate this knowledge as you make new connections to establish yourself as a professional expert.

There has been a significant amount written about the ideal client profile which can become your ideal prospect profile. The characteristics which will be important to you will vary based on what you are selling. Here is a partial list of characteristics to consider when creating your profiles:

- Company Overview
  - Revenue and Profitability
  - Number of Employees
  - Number of Locations (Local, National, and International)
  - Growth Mode (Expanding or Contracting)
- Industry

---

[6] Kotler, P. (2005, May 6). *According to Kotler: The World's Foremost Authority on Marketing Answers Your Questions*. AMACOM.

- Type (Public, Private, Non-Profit, or Government)
- Decision-making and Procurement Process
  - Centralized – utilizing strategic sourcing and perhaps a Request for Proposal (RFP) process with set contract periods
  - Decentralized – local management decides, and the process may vary
- Business and Investment Strategy
  - Cutting Edge – willing to make strategic investments and be first to market
  - Laggard – slow to invest in new technologies or systems
- Systems or Processes Utilized
  - The 'how' they produce what they offer or sell – manufacturer, reseller, or trader

You should certainly use the ones from this list that make the most sense, as well as incorporate other characteristics related to your specific industry and clients. Remember, you are trying to paint a picture of what your best clients look like so that you can compare that image to other companies you may consider approaching. The target accounts which best match this ideal client image should be at the top of your list. You will call on and sell your solution to other businesses as well. It is just a matter of prioritizing your time and understanding where you should ideally focus your efforts for maximum return.

A word about starting out when you are new to sales, with a new company, or in a new industry. While your enthusiasm to jump right in is fantastic, you need to recognize that you have not mastered all facets of the business. It might seem to make sense to approach the very best target accounts first. Perfectly logical. Except, it would be like fielding a team and then playing The Super Bowl first. Probably not the best idea if you want to achieve long-term success. Instead, I would suggest that you start with some of the companies which may not be an ideal match. It is the equivalent to playing a few pre-season games where the outcome does not impact your overall record. This will give you an opportunity to 'warm-up' before you go after the top prospects. Worst case, you will make calls on these less than perfect prospects and commit some mistakes. No worries. Sometimes you win and sometimes you **learn**. Initially, learning is more important than making a sale. And, who knows, you may even generate some sales through these activities as you are learning. Consider this a bonus. Either way it will provide you a chance to fine tune your approach, evaluate your sales process, and experience the buying and decision-making process in action. You will also learn more about your new industry and how your product or service creates value for a client. Once you have warmed-up, you can work your way up the target list, playing regular season games on the way to the play-offs, and eventually the title game. The purpose of this process is to identify, engage, and sell to the most favorable buyers.[7]

Learning Points:

1. Be sure to understand your territory assignment, whether it is a list of accounts, a defined geography, or some combination. Know the rules of engagement to ensure you do not work on any

---

[7] Porter, M.E. (1998, June 1). *Competitive Strategy: Techniques for Analyzing Industries and Competitors*. Free Press.

opportunities you will not earn you revenue or commission credit.

2. Develop an ideal client profile to understand which companies may need your product or service. Use this as a guide to evaluate and rank other businesses that might need what you offer. This will allow you to maximize your time and work on the best opportunities once you are properly prepared.

3. Take the opportunity to practice on less-than-ideal prospects to fine tune your approach. You will learn more about your own products and services, what your clients really value, and the role of competition in your industry. You may win some deals, but, more importantly, you will learn so you can improve for long term success.

"If you are not taking care of your customer, your competitor will."

Bob Hooey

"Never mistake activity for achievement."

John Wooden

Chapter 5: Calendar Management

There has been a significant amount written about time and calendar management. It is probably one of the most important skills to being a successful sales professional. Here is a simple truth you need to remember: time is your most valuable resource. It is a fixed and limited resource. We have only 24 hours each day and must maximize our return on investment. It is the one thing you must manage and use wisely to ensure you are investing your time in the activities that will generate the greatest results. It is all about return on investment. Never confuse being busy with achieving results. Everyone claims to be **busy,** but few can articulate what they **accomplished** today. Focus on accomplishing those things which will deliver the best results for your efforts and time investment.

Here is another truth. If you do not manage your time, you will discover other people are very willing to do that for you, and not always for your betterment. You will get invited to attend all kinds of meetings or events not focused on generating revenue. As Warren Buffet commented, "The difference between successful people and really successful people is that really successful people say no to almost everything." While some tasks are a part of any work environment, your ability to minimize these disruptions and work as efficiently as possible is critical. Your main job is to find, develop, and close business which generates revenue for your company and commission for you. Do not be afraid to say 'no'. Let people know you respect their time, as well as your time, and find other ways to engage with and handle non-essential tasks efficiently to protect your selling time. Offer to speak to people while you are traveling to and from appointments in the car rather than coming into the office during the middle of the day. When an in-person meeting is necessary, work to schedule it early or late in the day, to preserve the central part of your day for activities that generate sales success.

I would recommend using an electronic calendar which is integrated into your Customer Relationship Management (CRM) system if available. This will help you track your activities, often without having to enter activities multiple times, as well as provide members of your team easy access to your schedule. We will discuss the importance of developing a support team in Chapter 18. Suffice it to say that it is essential for your support team to have access to your daily planner so they know where you are and when you will be available to meet with prospects or clients. You should also understand if there are ways to integrate your phone into the CRM system for quicker updates on the go. Anything which can save you time is something you want to learn about and utilize.

There is a great deal of information available on time management. If this is an area that you find personally challenging, you may want to do some additional research or register for a class to get additional support. The information here is to provide you with some general best practices and ideas to leverage your time to maximize your results. These are strategies I have used over the years for myself, as well as leading many sales professionals, to help improve and excel. You should also remember that as you develop, and you become more proficient and successful, you will want to become even more selective about where you invest your time. In the beginning, you will take appointments with semi-qualified prospects because you don't have any other choices. As you build your business, you will be able to spend your time with the best prospects working on the most lucrative opportunities.

Color Code Your Calendar

Your calendar allows you to plan and record the details of all your activities. However, you can increase the effectiveness of this tool by taking advantage of color coding your activities to provide a quick visual representation of how you are investing your time each day. You should be able to glance at your calendar and see the most important activities vividly. If you do not see the most important activities at a glance, you should stop and ask yourself what's going on. What is on your calendar other than the activities most likely to drive revenue and commissions? Take the appropriate action to invest your time where it will generate the greatest results. Here are some suggestions to get you started.

Green: Prospect or Client-Facing Sales Appointments

Green is the color of money. Your calendar should be filled with green if you want your pockets lined with money. You can even use two shades of green to denote the difference between an existing client meeting (dark green) and a new prospect meeting (bright green) so you can ensure a good mix of these two critical activities.

Blue: Networking Events

This includes lead-sharing group meetings, trade associations, business networking functions, as well as one-on-one meetings to cultivate relationships and foster new opportunities. Organic development of new opportunities is critical even if your company provides you leads. Organic refers to the leads and opportunities you develop and not leads or opportunities that are provided by your employer. You can never have too many opportunities in the works.

Yellow: Proactive Telemarketing or Cold-calling Activities

You should always dedicate time each week to call prospects and clients to check in and offer something of value. Too little time is dedicated to using the phone to sell.[8] It is certainly one of the most efficient ways to speak with a broad range of prospects and clients efficiently. It will allow you to uncover new information and schedule online and face-to-face appointments as appropriate.

Orange: Mandatory Internal Meetings or Activities

These are the 'must do' items. While you cannot always control these meetings, you should work to minimize their impact on your calendar. Where possible, push back. At the very least, encourage those scheduling these activities to keep them early or late to protect the key selling hours of your day.

---

[8] Goldfayn, A. (2021, Sept. 22). *Pick Up The Phone and Sell: How Proactive Calls to Customers and Prospects Can Double Your Sales*. Wiley.

Red: 'To Do's and Reminders

These are items with a definitive due date. When possible, use the task or 'to-do' function inside your CRM tool to capture prospect and client-related activities. Sometimes these functions can be displayed on your calendar for easy reference. This is also a great way to set reminders for submitting reports, time sheets, expenses, and anything else you are supposed to do on a regular basis which can slip your mind. Remember, these are often the little things that drive sales manager crazy – so stay on top of them.

Remember, this is just a suggested list. You can certainly add other colors to denote a whole host of other professional, and even personal appointments, to manage your time wisely and effectively. Most electronic calendars allow you to name the activity for each color selected. The important thing to remember is that you want to see your calendar with plenty of Green, Blue, and Yellow. These are selling and revenue-generating activities. They should constitute the bulk of each workday. Other activities should be relegated to non-selling hours when possible. In general, you want to keep your calendar clear from 9:00 AM to 3:00

PM to be engaged in productive selling engagements. Protect your time as it is your most valuable resource.

Maximize Every Appointment

It is wonderful when you have prospects and clients who are willing to meet with you. You will certainly want to schedule as many appointments as possible. In-person visits are among the best ways to build a relationship, learn, and promote the value of your offering. However, depending on the size of your territory, or if you must travel to in-person meetings, you will want to be careful to avoid become a 'star' salesperson. The 'star' moniker, in this situation, is not a good distinction. It represents the shape on a map of someone who spends their entire day crisscrossing the roads and highways, going from meeting to meeting. You should be diligent to group meetings by location to maximize your selling time and minimize your travel time. This is especially true if you have long distance travel requiring overnight trips.

While this may appear intuitive, many sales professionals are so happy to get an appointment, they let the client make all the decisions about when to meet. It really is not that difficult to find some common ground if you simply ask politely. For example, let's say you are speaking with a prospect who agrees to see you. He is located near another appointment you have on Thursday at 11:00 AM. You can simply say, "I appreciate your willingness to meet with me. I will be near your office this coming Thursday. Would you be available to see me at 9:30 AM, or would 1:00 PM be more convenient?" Always offer a choice. Let them be in 'control' as you steer them towards the desired result. This same strategy can work in other ways as well. If you were going to be nearby on Thursday or the following Monday, you could ask, "Would you prefer to meet this Thursday, or would Monday be more convenient?" A good follow up question would be, "Would you prefer to meet in the morning or the afternoon on that day?" or perhaps, "Would 1:30 PM be acceptable or would 2:30 PM be more convenient for your schedule?" Always provide a choice so you get a 'yes' to your request since either choice selected is a win for you.

Appointment 'Wings'©

I have lead sales teams for many years and one of the most productive techniques cultivated is the concept of putting 'wings' on appointments.© When conducting one-on-one reviews with a sales professional, we make a point to review their calendar for the upcoming week. Inevitably we notice some appointments, but often there is white space where they have nothing scheduled. We look at a specific appointment, let's say at 11:00 AM on Monday, and I ask them how we can put some wings on this appointment. For example, if you are traveling downtown to meet with a prospect at 11:00 AM, are there any clients along the way, or nearby, who you could visit? What about a competitive account? Perhaps it is an opportunity to quickly deliver a token gift with a handwritten note requesting a future visit? What about networking partners? Is there anyone you have wanted to build a stronger relationship you could invite to coffee beforehand, or lunch afterwards? Perhaps there is a building or two you have wanted to visit to conduct some cold calls. Be creative to see what potential interactions can be scheduled in the time allotted to assist you in developing new relationships and new opportunities.

When you are reviewing your calendar at the end of the week for the coming week, print out a copy and start adding boxes before and after each scheduled appointment as noted below. These boxes are the 'wings'. Now start to think of ways to multiply your effectiveness. If you have six appointments scheduled this week, and can add two wings to each, you will triple the number of people you see this week. Triple. You will go from six to 18 interactions with just a little effort. If you average six appointments a week, and utilize this technique, over the course of a year, you will generate more than **600** additional opportunities to make a connection or build a relationship. It is the equivalent of working one hundred extra weeks a year, given an average weekly call rate of six appointments.

Depending on your business and industry, you may find that you can add more than two wings onto each scheduled appointment. Perhaps you can stop by and see two prospects instead of one. That would be an additional **300** additional opportunities a year for a total of **900**. You can see how powerful this evolution in mindset could be to your business. Each additional opportunity has an exponential impact and will greatly increase the odds of your future success. Some activity will be centered around initiating or building relationships while others will be centered around identifying new opportunities. Each is required to give your business balance, and both should be relentlessly pursued. No matter how busy you are you must always schedule time for business development activities.

If you have a geographic territory assignment, gaining access to certain buildings, in today's climate, can be a challenge given heightened security concerns. Some buildings will deny you access unless you have a stated purpose, such as a confirmed appointment, with a tenant. In some locations, you cannot simply walk in and start making cold calls. When you have an appointment scheduled at a specific location, check the building tenant list for any other companies you may want to visit while you are there. You will be able to go to your scheduled appointment and then, on the way out, stop by other offices to make a traditional cold-call visit. While cold calling is not the most effective prospecting tool, when you are starting off it can be another method to initiate new connections and generate opportunities. In the beginning, you must start somewhere.

You may even want to make phone calls in advance to see if potential key contacts would be available for a brief introduction. I like the idea of requesting a 'visit' for a quick 'chat' rather than a 'meeting' for a 'discussion'. It is a more casual way of asking to see someone face-to-face. You may find you're able to increase your face-to-face selling time using this technique. If not, try stopping by their office to leave a handwritten note with your business card. It will be seen as a thoughtful gesture which may open the door to a future in-person meeting. Visit my website at www.practical-sales-wisdom.com for some specific examples you can use.

Remember, we are not stopping by to visit people just to be friendly. Whether we are visiting a prospect, client, or networking partner, we should have a reason or goal in mind for the visit. If we take time to visit a prospect to deliver some cookies and a handwritten note, the goal is to get a chance to introduce yourself and then request an in-person meeting. If we stop by a current client to visit, we should express our gratitude for their business and then look to see how we can expand our business relationship (improve our share of wallet). Perhaps we could ask for an introduction to someone else in the organization who purchases a product from a competitor. When we visit with a networking partner, we should bring a lead, or perhaps a strategic introduction suggestion, to help our partner build their business. You get by giving. Always be willing to give first. In each of these interactions there should be a goal to improve your business. Be strategic in your thinking, so you will uncover and develop more opportunities.

Do you think you will find some additional opportunities doing this? Absolutely. And it beats sitting in the office waiting for the phone to ring, with your sales manager glaring down at you. Here are some examples to illustrate the 'wings' concept.

Current Calendar View

Time	Mon	Tue	Wed	Thu	Fri
8					
9			MTG		
10	MTG				MTG
11					
12					
1		MTG			
2				MTG	
3					
4					
5					

Calendar View with Wings

Time	Mon	Tue	Wed	Thu	Fri
8			5		
9	1		MTG		9
10	MTG		6		MTG
11	2				10
12		3			
1		MTG		7	
2		4		MTG	
3				8	
4					
5					

Learning Points:

1. Time is your most valuable resource. Protect your time by instituting a solid approach to managing your calendar in order to maximize your selling time. Use color coding to ensure your calendar is full of the most important types of activities – those that lead to revenue generation.

2. Plan your time to minimize windshield (driving) time. Consolidate appointments in one or two geographic areas each day. Avoid being a 'star' salesperson.

3. Put wings on your appointments to create additional opportunities to meet with prospects, clients, and networking partners. Turn each appointment into an opportunity to visit with two or three other people and watch your relationships and business grow.

4. "Get busy and then get expensive" (Unknown). When you are starting off, you will be less selective in order to learn and start to build your business. As you get more proficient, you will be busy and able to charge a

premium for your products and services. Remember, you are part of the experience someone is buying.

"The difference between try and triumph is just the amount of 'umph' added to the try."

Roy Johnsen

"Keep your sales prospecting pipeline full by prospecting continuously. Always have more people to see than you have time to see them."

Brian Tracy

Chapter 6: Opportunity Management

As I mentioned, I am fond of the statement by Mike Weinberg, from his book, *New Sales. Simplified.*, that says sales professionals have three primary responsibilities: to create new opportunities, to advance opportunities, and to close opportunities.[9] It's simple, but true. This is the reason businesses hire top sales talent. Sales professionals are the ones whose mission is to drive revenue, win business, and generate profits. A key component of accomplishing this goal is the proper management of your opportunities. This is often referred to as pipeline management or forecasting. No matter the moniker, the key concepts remain the same. It is the ability to develop new opportunities, track their

---

[9] Weinberg. M. (2012, Sept. 4). *New Sales. Simplified.: The Essential Handbook for Prospecting and New Business Development*. AMACOM.

progress through the sales cycle, and eventually win the business. Here we will review some basic truths about opportunity management.

You may utilize a CRM system which has a system to track your opportunities. If not, you might consider a simple spreadsheet to accomplish the same result. No matter the system, you will want to manage each opportunity. I say 'manage' because this is an activity. You cannot allow your pipeline to be in a passive mode where deals are expected to take care of themselves. They will eventually take care of themselves by ending up in the 'lost' column. You need to be engaged, every day, with your pipeline. As a matter of fact, I recommend that you have a weekly appointment on your calendar to do a systematic review of your pipeline to ensure you have enough opportunities in each phase of development to generate a steady stream of revenue and commissions. There is a direct correlation between effective opportunity management and generating a strong revenue stream.[10]

On a most basic level, you will need to identify some key information for each opportunity. The amount of information may be different based on the specific requirements of your organization and your CRM system. Be sure to follow the process and provide the necessary information. For our purposes, here is a basic example:

Company Name:	ABC Company
Point of Contact:	Mr. Prospect
Email:	prospect@abc.com
Address:	123 Prospect Ave.
Targeted Product/Service:	Widget 101
Current Product/Service:	Competitor Name
Value:	$10,000
Estimated Close Date:	12/1/2022
Status:	Discovery

---

[10] Samoisette, M. (2018, Nov. 5). *Sales Processified: How Small Business CEOs Can Implement a Sales Process That Gets Results.* Elevate Coaching Press.

Now, this is a single opportunity. Your pipeline will consist of many opportunities in various phases of the sales cycle with varying probabilities of success. No matter how this information is organized, there are some fundamental principles you will want to keep in mind to master opportunity management. Elite sales professionals keep a careful eye on their pipeline to ensure they have an ample supply of opportunities in every phase of the sales cycle. So, if your typical sales cycle is 90 to 120 days in length, you will need to have enough opportunities closing this month, next month, and so on. It is a rolling month-to-month process that requires you have enough opportunities in each phase of development to close each coming month.

When a sales professional doesn't have any business to close in a particular month, it generally isn't something they did, or did not do, in that specific month. Most likely, it was something they didn't do 90 to 150 days prior (if their sales cycles generally run between 90 to 120 days). The seeds you plant today will grow the fruit you will harvest in the future. Make sure you are always planting and caring for your future harvest.

For example, if you have 10 opportunities with six deciding this month, and three deciding next month, and one the following month, you have a problem if your sales cycle is 90 to 120 days long. Setting aside the value and the probability of each, you have a diminishing number of deals to work after the current month. Given the time it takes to develop a new opportunity, even if you find a new opportunity today, it will be three to four months before it will be 'ripe' for the picking. This will leave you a gap of several months where you may not be generating any sales.

Here is an example. If your typical sales cycle, from start to decision, is 90 to 120 days in length, any new opportunity you find on January 1st will most likely not be ready to buy until April or May. What are you going to sell in January, February, and March? You need to be constantly adding new valid opportunities to have a steady stream of deals ready to close on a consistent monthly basis.

This is an area where a typical salesperson's performance suffers. They get busy working on a few good opportunities and neglect to add anything new. Even if they close the business they are working on, by the time they get prospecting again, they run into a slump because their pipeline ran dry. This is another difference between regular salespeople and high-performing sales professionals. The high-performing sales professionals are continually adding newly qualified opportunities to their pipeline while making sure the opportunities already identified are progressing along to close. Remember, business development should be a part of what you do every day. You always want to be cultivating new opportunities so you can perform at a high level on a consistent basis. Here are some basic rules for properly managing your opportunities.

Pipeline Rule #1: Pipeline Integrity

It is essential that the opportunities you have listed in your pipeline are real: you have met with the prospect, understand their needs, have a viable solution to offer that will create value, and understand how they can buy from you. It means you have properly qualified this prospect and will have a real opportunity to do business together.

I have seen it many times where salespeople put nearly anyone with a pulse in their pipeline. As soon as a lead comes in, it's an opportunity. Yes, in the traditional sense, every lead is an opportunity, but not every opportunity should be in your pipeline. Limit inclusion to those opportunities that you have properly qualified. The challenge with having unqualified opportunities in your pipeline is that it makes it difficult to focus on your most valid deals. Yes, more opportunities are better, but only if they are valid. Clarity is important. Don't lose track of the important trees because they exist in a cluttered forest.

Pipeline Rule #2: Probability of Winning the Business

Some CRM systems have a scoring system to calculate the probability of an opportunity turning into business based on where you are in the sales process. These tools can be very helpful. However, I have found you can also focus on a simple sliding scale to score each opportunity that will help you determine the next step in advancing and eventually closing the business.

Here is the scale:

25%: Low Probability of Winning

50%: Medium Probability of Winning

75%: High Probability of Winning

100%: Verbal Commitment from the Economic Buyer

It is essential to apply honest scores to each opportunity to know where you currently stand. Again, you need to be brutally honest with yourself. While I appreciate optimism, this is not the time to be optimistic. It is a time to be honest.

An opportunity at a 25%-win rate is one that is highly competitive, and you are not in the lead position. Most likely this is a new prospect rather than an existing account, where you are trying to unseat a competitor. While you have been engaged, you recognize the decision influencers are not totally onboard or seem to favor another option. You may have been unable to establish a coach/champion who can guide you or provide essential insights into the buying and decision-making process. Essentially, you are in the game, but trailing with the clock ticking down.

An opportunity at a 50%-win rate is also competitive situation but one where you have an equal chance at winning the business. This might be with either a new prospect or existing client where there are multiple stakeholders with varying degrees of influence. You may have a coach or champion who is able to provide insights but is unable to exert enough influence to ensure you are in the lead position. Essentially, you are in a dog fight but with a fair shot of winning.

An opportunity at a 75%-win rate is leaning your way. Perhaps it is with an existing client who favors you and your company. Perhaps it is with a new account where you have developed a good relationship with the decision influencers and/or the economic buyer. You may even have a coach/champion who regularly provides you an inside view and is optimistic you are in the lead position. Essentially, you are the lead horse coming around the third pole.

An opportunity at a 100%-win rate is one where you have received a verbal commitment from the economic buyer. While the contract has not been signed, you have been told that a decision has been made in your favor and now they need to complete the contracting. Remember, this is not a done deal. Many opportunities have been lost during the last steps in securing the proper contracting. However, you have heard from the person who can say 'yes' that you have won the business. Essentially, this is your deal to lose.

Pipeline Rule #3: "The What Question"©

Now that you have a list of opportunities and applied some win probability rate to each, the real fun begins. This is where you get to ask yourself one of the most important questions in opportunity management: The What Question

©. "What could I do today to improve my opportunity to win the business?" This is, in essence, the concept of advancing the opportunity forward. However, every opportunity is different, and each is also in a different phase. You need to think about what you could do today to move an opportunity from a 25%-win rate to a 50%-win rate or a 50%-win rate to a 75%-win rate.

This does not have to be a solo adventure. One of the great things about this process is bringing in your sales manager, a teammate, or another trusted advisor to strategize and brainstorm with you. It is about being *proactive* rather than *reactive*. It is totally possible that an opportunity you never thought you would win ends up buying from you. Yes, a blind squirrel occasionally finds a nut. But that doesn't make it a best practice. While we accept luck when it comes, it is not a sound strategy overall. You need to be proactive in all your activities, especially managing your pipeline.

Pipeline Rule #4: Act Now!

Once you have reviewed each opportunity and determined a viable next step, go do it. Now, let me be clear. I'm not suggesting you randomly call each prospect and ask, "Have you made a decision yet?" While that is proactive, it probably won't help your situation. I'm suggesting you develop a specific strategic action that will improve your standing. Each situation will be different, and it will require you being a strategic thinker. Here are a few general suggestions to prime your creative thinking:

1. *Provide a Positive Reference*

   Perhaps you are working with someone who is not yet convinced of the value you claim you can create. You might be able to ask an existing client who is a raving fan to either call or write an email to your prospect sharing their positive experiences and recommending you. While your prospect may not have explicitly asked for a reference, they may welcome the opportunity to hear from someone familiar with you and your company to validate your value creation claims.

2. Send A Review

If your product, service, or company recently received third-party recognition, like an award or accolade, consider sending this information to your prospect. Or perhaps your product was just compared to similar products in a reputable journal and received a very positive review. The more it relates to their specific situation the better. However, any positive news about your organization may promote a more positive image and help nudge the opportunity forward.

3. Schedule a Visit to Chat

You could call the prospect and say, "I want to make sure that I am creating the most value for your personally, and for your company, with the recommendation provided. However, I feel as if there might be something missing. Do you have a few minutes for us to chat?" This question will also qualify where you are in the process. If the prospect agrees to meet, they might be willing to share some new information with you or express some legitimate concerns you need to address. If they refuse to meet because they are comfortable with your recommendation, you may well learn where you stand. Even if the news is 'bad', you win. Because now you know for certain where you are and can either take additional action or move on.

4. *Offer a Site Tour or Demonstration*

If you sell a service, offer to take the prospect to visit an existing client to see how your offering adds value. If you sell a product, offer a demonstration or on-site trial. If the prospect is unable to attend either in person, offer to schedule a virtual tour or demonstration using video conferencing technology. Let them know you appreciate the challenge in selecting the best partner for the project, and you would appreciate the opportunity to show them the value you can create for them. Use your creativity to demonstrate your commitment to earning the business while your competitors wait for their phone to ring.

These are just a few ideas of taking action to progress the opportunity to the next stage and eventually to captured business. You can certainly add or modify these ideas as needed. However, make sure that there is action. Don't simply wait to see what will happen. Create your own desired outcome by taking positive action today.

If your current CRM system has win probability intelligence incorporated or measures potential success by where you are in the sales process, you should use that technology. Instead of the scale presented above, simply use the scale built into the system. The steps outlined remain the same. For each opportunity as yourself the "What Question"© and see how you can improve your chances of advancing the sale or winning the business today. Then act now. Don't hesitate to do something today to improve your chances of winning the business.

Your Batting Average

As a high-performing sales professional, you will want to track your batting average. Simply stated, this is your win-to-loss ratio. For example, if you were working 10 valid opportunities in January, and you won six and lost four, you would be batting .600 or have a 60%-win rate. The validity of this information requires sufficient time to look at a true run rate. However, you also need to consider the value of each opportunity if you sell a variety of products or services with different values. For example, if you sell a range of products with varying price points, you may want to evaluate the win percentage from a revenue perspective. As in our previous example, you were working on 10 opportunities with a total value of $100,000. You won six valued at $60,000 and lost four valued at $40,000, you have a .600 batting average or a 60%-win rate. However, this can get tricky if the value of the six deals you won were only worth $40,000 while the four deals you lost were worth $60,000. Now your batting average would only be .400 equivalent to a 40%-win rate. In either case this is useful information to help you track your progress. You may even want to break this information down further by the size of the deals, if there is a widespread in the price points, or by existing and net new business. Net New Business refers to a sale to a new customer, someone who is not currently, or has not recently, purchased from your company.

In either scenario, it is a good idea to track your monthly results to understand your personal batting average. This will be especially useful when you are required to submit a forecast, or a commitment, for the coming month or quarter. A forecast is generally a formal process for most companies where you are required to state what you will sell the next month. It may require you to list each opportunity and the value. In addition to that commitment, you might be asked to identify any 'upside' or other deals that might come to fruition in the same month. Upside is an opportunity you might be able to win but is not strong enough to commit to winning. When creating your forecast, you will want to have an ample supply of upside opportunities to cover any misses in the committed category or to be additional revenue you can deliver for the company and yourself.

Many organizations take forecasting very seriously. It is your 'promise' to your manager, and the entire sales management hierarchy, of the revenue you will generate. Companies use this information for various purposes, including setting expectations with senior management, ownership, a board of directors, and even banks and investors. You will want to ensure your forecast is accurate and that you (at a minimum) "hit" your commitment. My advice is to be conservative in your estimates and make sure you achieve or exceed your commitment on a regular basis. There is nothing worse than a sales professional who cannot predict what revenue they will generate each month. It's a fundamental responsibility of your job to accurately know this information.

Learning Points:

1. It is critical to develop and actively manage your opportunities. Remember, your job is to create opportunities, advance opportunities, and close opportunities.[11]

---

[11] Weinberg. M. (2012, Sept. 4). *New Sales. Simplified.: The Essential Handbook for Prospecting and New Business Development.* AMACOM.

2. Use a system to score each opportunity to understand the probability of winning the business. Be brutally honest. This is no time for optimism. You need an honest assessment of each opportunity so you can proactively manage it.

3. Ask yourself the "What Question"© for each opportunity in your pipeline: "What could I do today to improve my opportunity to win the business?" Use your creativity and the suggestions provided to find something that will advance the opportunity in the sales process to a successful conclusion.

4. Understand your batting average. Utilize your CRM system or another tool to track you wins and losses so you can gauge your effectiveness over time. In most cases you will find that as you become more proficient and confident in your abilities your win percentage will improve. The goal is to get better day by day.

5. Forecasting is a commitment you make to yourself, your manager, and the leadership of the company. Make sure you are accurate and conservative in your

commitments. Let the revenue generated speak for itself.

"The first key to greatness is to be in reality what we appear to be."

Socrates

"Practice is just as valuable as a sale. The sale will make you a living; the skill will make you a fortune."

Jim Rohn

Chapter 7: Learning is Key

When you begin your first sales position, it is critical to learn as much as you can as rapidly as you can. This will include what is expected of you, the technical specifications of the products and services you offer, the industry and the competition, as well as the target market, among other items. It is a great deal to absorb in a short period of time. I will write from the perspective of someone very new to a company, but the concepts can also be used by those who have been in their current role for some time. One of the biggest mistakes a new sales professional can make is letting their enthusiasm for getting out there overpower the time they should initially invest in learning. I am not opposed to enthusiasm. Enthusiasm is essential to success. However, do not be in such a rush to hit the streets until you have taken the time to educate yourself sufficiently to be competent and effective.

Some organizations do an excellent job of presenting this information to new hires. They have extensive resources, perhaps they even have professional trainers on staff, who engage new sales professionals with textbooks, videos, and in-person learning events to impart this important information. They may even test for understanding and engage in role-playing exercises, creating scenarios to apply this knowledge in practice. Some organizations even send new hires to a school to learn about the business in greater detail, as well as to receive additional sales training. If you work for this type of organization, you are fortunate. Take advantage of every opportunity. However, as I have learned, many organizations are not large enough, or sophisticated enough, to offer this level of training. Their size and scope do not permit these dedicated resources. In most instances, the sales manager is the person responsible for developing the onboarding plan and for getting a new hire up to speed. In these cases, you will experience a wide range of effectiveness. Once again, I encourage you to maximize the opportunities presented. You might, however, want to consider the following to supplement and strengthen the onboarding process and to provide yourself a launching pad to jumpstart your sales success.

You will want to distinguish between developing your sales acumen and learning the technical and functional parts of your business. By technical I mean everything that has to do with the actual products and/or services you will be selling. It is important to learn about them in detail and how they differ from what your competitors offer. Buyers select business partners based on the understanding they demonstrate of the industry and unique business issues.[12] Buyers today want to work with businesspeople who can identify the right problems and help them solve those problems, not simply salespeople who are only interested in selling a product or service.

---

[12] Stein, D. & Anderson, S. (2016, April 4). *Beyond the Sales Process: 12 Proven Strategies for a Customer-Driven World*. AMACOM.

By functional I mean the 'ins and outs' of how the work is done. Everything from completing your time sheet, to submitting an expense report, to placing an order for a client. Here you may have the opportunity to work with a client success representative, operations, order fulfillment, accounting, and others who assist in doing the work. It is essential to learn these processes so you can be as efficient as possible. Further, you want to develop a reputation as a team player. A team player is a person who contributes to the overall success of the organization. You will have difficulty emulating this persona if you cannot navigate the fundamental functions of your job. The more you do your part well, the better others can do their part well. You do not want to earn a reputation as being difficult to work with when it is so easy to be a good teammate. You will also find that some of these people are ideal candidates for your Internal Support Team – a concept we will discuss in greater detail in Chapter 18.

Current Clients

Most sales professionals are assigned a territory that defines their responsibilities. Generally, a territory consists of both existing clients as well as prospects. A careful examination of your existing client base is an important first step in learning. Yes, learning. Learning is more important than running out and trying to sell these clients more. I recognize this appears counterintuitive, but as I explain the process, the reasoning should become clear.

You might be thinking that your client list offers an excellent opportunity to sell more to the people who are already doing business with your company. You are correct. You will certainly want to engage these buyers to sell them more ancillary products and services. What I recommend though is that you take a step back and let them educate you first. As we know, they are doing business with your company, which tells me they are pleased with what you are providing them. For all intents and purposes, they are happy customers. Perfect. These are exactly the type of people you will want to speak with initially. They will be able to provide you important insights about your company, your products, or services, and the best way to approach **prospective** clients to demonstrate the value you can create for them.

The goal here is to contact the current clients you have been assigned and request a brief visit to introduce yourself and chat for a few minutes. Let them know that you are genuinely interested in being a resource for them and you want to initiate a relationship with them to best serve their needs. In most cases, you will find clients very willing to meet with you to talk about their favorite subject – themselves. This will give you the opportunity to listen to them in detail and learn about their personality. This will also provide you the opportunity to start building a solid relationship with your key clients.

They may expect you to come in, introduce yourself, and then launch into some pitch about your newest products or why they should upgrade their current equipment to something new. In other words, they are going to be a little guarded at first. The key in the first few minutes is to start to build a connection. I would recommend this as a guide:

1. Introduction
2. Thank you for your business – we appreciate you!

3. I was wondering if you could help me.

The third item, "I was wondering if you could help me?" is the main point. Here you want to wait for the client to consider your request and answer in the affirmative. It is only then that you can move to the next step, which is to state, "I am new to XYZ Company and the industry in general. I was hoping you might be willing to share some of your experiences as a way for me to learn more about the business?" Simple and straight to the point. I think you will find most people willing to answer your questions. Quite frankly, most people enjoy being the expert and distilling their knowledge to others. If you just ask nicely, you would be amazed at how helpful most people are willing to be.

When they acknowledge your question and agree to share their experiences with you, be sure to ask, "Would you mind if I took some notes?" This is important for several reasons. First, it will signify respect to the client. You value their guidance and want to make sure you write it down, so you will not forget. Second, it will have an impact on how they interface with you. Beyond seeing that you are genuinely interested in learning their perspective, you will find they will be more thoughtful with the information they provide, and they will speak more slowly in recognition of you taking notes. This is the same reason I always ask this question during the discovery phase. I have never had anyone deny this simple request.

Some clients might launch right into information while others might require a prompt. While you want this to be a genuine conversation, do not be afraid to let them know you have prepared a few questions to guide the discussion. It will let them know you are a professional and respect their time. It is a practice which will serve you well whenever you are meeting with someone. Consider the following questions as a starting point for your inquiry:

1. Why do you do business with my company?
2. What do we do well? Where could we improve?
3. Who did you do business with before us? What, if anything, prompted you to switch providers?

4. How did you decide to select our company? What is the process your company uses to make these types of decisions?

5. What organizations do you belong to? How do you keep current on industry trends?

6. What are your priorities for the balance of the year? Is there anything I can do to be of assistance to you?

Let us look at each question and clearly understand what we are trying to gain from the discussion. Remember, this is a learning opportunity.

Why do you do business with my company?

This question appears simplistic, but it is designed to uncover what motivates the client to give your company their money. They have lots of choices. Why is your company preferred to others in the market offering similar if not an identical solution? You want to hear about this from their perspective because they are like other buyers you will be approaching in the near future. By understanding the rationale of your current clients, you will be able to use this insight to engage prospects in a meaningful discussion about your offering and the value you can create for them. It will allow you to demonstrate your expertise and true business acumen. Again, it will allow you to differentiate yourself in a crowded marketplace.

For example, the client may say they find your product extremely reliable, or a great value, or easy to use. Write that down. It is important. But the follow up question is even more important. And that question is either how or why. You want to drill down to understand why the client provided this specific insight. So, for example, if the client says, "Your product is reliable," follow up by asking, "How is reliability important to you?" or "How does reliability impact your business?" While they identified a benefit your product or service offers, how it impacts them, and their business, is even more important. They might say, "it saves me time" or "it saves us money." Again, drill down a little deeper to understand why that is important or by obtaining more specific details. "How much time does it save you per day (or week or month)?" or "How much money is it saving you daily (weekly or monthly)?" This information will allow you to develop compelling opening statements when working to open a conversation or secure an appointment with a prospect at another company. Therefore, you want to ensure a complete understanding so you can really have a professional conversation with a prospect about their business.

When people are deciding whether to buy from you, there are several factors involved in that decision. The first key factor is how it will impact them, personally, and second, how it will impact their business. You would expect there to be perfect alignment here, but that is not always the case. People buy for their reasons, not yours. The better you become at recognizing their motivations the better you will be able to properly position your solution to maximize the value to them as well as their company.

The key here is to dig down until you hit bedrock. Do not simply accept the first thing they offer without understanding the impact to them personally and to their business. These are the real reasons they bought from your company, and they may be the very reason other prospects would be motivated to buy from you if you were able to clearly articulate these benefits to them. Further, while you may assume how being more reliable helps them, it is only your opinion. When the client states the reason, it is a fact. We want to operate in the world of facts.

What do we do well? Where could we improve?

Here you want to discover more about what it is like to interface with your company. What is the buyer experience from their perspective? What do they like best and what could use some improvement? Just like with the first question, you will want to drill down to get to the underlying meaning of what is being conveyed. When you are asking these questions, do not debate or offer excuses. You should focus on extracting the information only at this point, even if what they tell you is incomplete or erroneous from your perspective. Save that discussion for another time.

For example, the client may say, "Your customer service is good." Fantastic, we are always glad to hear that. Follow up with, "What specifically makes our customer service good?" or "Who do you call when you need assistance?" or "Who goes above and beyond to assist you?" as well as "How does this make your life easier?" or "How does this help your business?" Get as much specific information as possible and take good notes. They are telling you, from their perspective, what they find valuable and advantageous working with your company. These are the benefits they realize being a client, and this is information you can share with prospects.

When you ask about how you might improve, listen carefully to the unspoken thoughts. If the client says, "I wish you could deliver faster" or "I wish the invoicing were easier to understand," the client is giving you fresh information about how you can improve the relationship, their interaction with your company, and how you can ensure their continued loyalty. You do not want to jump up and scream "I can fix that!" even if you can. Instead, make a note and ask more questions to fully understand the problem. Your ability to eventually solve the issue is an opportunity to strengthen and solidify the relationship with the client. But first you must learn more about the impact of the problem. You want to potentially solve a significant problem and not just a small inconvenience. Again, probe the client about why these things are important and gain a clear understanding as to how an improvement in this area might impact them personally, their business, and your relationship.

Let us take the example of, "I wish you could deliver faster." This comment could be based on any number of factors and might be solved using a more creative approach to the problem. For example, the client might use your product in the manufacture of their product. Your product is an essential input. They use a variable number of your products each month depending on orders they receive from their customers. However, your client never reorders until they are nearly out of stock. When they run out completely it causes a serious delay in their manufacturing process. You could offer several solutions to assist. Perhaps by automating the process with shipments scheduled in advance to avoid shortfalls. Or maybe you could reach out each month and remind the client to check the inventory levels to ensure they place the order in time for delivery before it negatively impacts their business. Maybe there is someone in their shop that your customer service representative could check in with every few weeks to monitor the consumption levels to ensure orders are placed timely to avoid future delays.

There are certainly several approaches to properly addressing this concern. But before you jump in and solve the problem, be sure to identify the impact on them and their business. You want the solution to generate value. The bigger the problem, the greater the value in solving the problem. You want to maximize the impact of the solution so that you will be viewed as a valuable resource and eventually a trusted advisor. A trusted advisor is defined as someone who is "given a seat at the customer's table. Instead of being just another vendor...you're considered a strategic partner that the customer sees as an asset to reach their goals."[13]

Let us also remember that delivery delays might be a reason for the client to switch providers and start doing business with one of your competitors. While the overall relationship is good right now, they might not recognize their poor planning is the issue rather than the perception that your delivery process is slow. People will likely look for external sources to explain a problem, rather than accepting responsibility. By addressing this problem, you are blocking a competitor from using it as an entry point to build a case for changing suppliers. Remember, every one of your clients is a prospect for one of your competitors. They want to steal your clients from you so they can earn the revenue and commissions for themselves. Client retention is as critical as securing new accounts. You want to maintain your client base as you add new clients (i.e., steal business and commissions from your competitors!).

---

[13] Raymond, A. (n.d.). *What Does It Mean to Be a Trusted Advisor?* Kapta. Retrieved Feb. 1, 2022, from https://kapta.com/resources/key-account-management-blog/key-account-management/mean-trusted-advisor

Who did you do business with before us? What, if anything, prompted you to switch providers?

Here you can learn about potential competitors and what they did well and what they did not do well. Change is difficult and most companies are slow to initiate change. If you have a client that went through the effort, they clearly saw benefits to acting. Learn what motivated them to change. What did they expect, and did they achieve their goals making the transition? Did they realize any additional benefits after they switched providers? If so, what were they and how are they important? This is information you will be able to use in developing specific and targeted value proposition statements for prospective clients who may be using the same former provider. It is the specificity of the information that makes it so powerful. You can be direct and accurate in your questions and statements, and not simply throw a guess against the wall, hoping it sticks when you start prospecting. Information is power and this knowledge will allow you to sound more competent and professional. It will also provide you a significant competitive advantage: "Competitive advantage refers to factors that allow a company to produce goods or services better or more cheaply than its rivals."[14]

How did you decide to select our company? What is the process your company uses for making these types of decisions?

It isn't a good idea to ask someone directly if they are the ultimate decision maker. It puts undue pressure on them. Either they really are, or they are not. If they're not, they might feel as if their standing is being questioned. I always find it better to ask about the decision-making process. This approach is less direct but will provide you the same information. For example, "How does your company make these types of decisions?" It is even less specific than asking about how they made this specific decision. It will still prompt the client to discuss who was involved, their roles, potential concerns, and the actual process for initiating a new contract if required. Again, you are trying to gain important insights into how they were thinking about the

[14] Twin, A. (2021, Mar. 8). *Competitive Advantage: What is a Competitive Advantage?* Investopedia. Retrieved from https://www.investopedia.com/terms/c/competitive_advantage.asp

decision to see how it might apply to other businesses like them.

What organizations do you belong to? How do you keep current on industry trends?

As we will discuss in Chapter 19, joining, and actively participating in, various industry or trade associations is a great way to gain access to key influencers and decision makers. Learn which groups your clients participate in. Ask about their meeting schedule and what they enjoy most about being a member. If they are enthusiastic about the group, ask if they are looking for new members (most are always looking for additional members). Ask if you could attend a meeting with them to learn more about their organization. Talk about relationship building!

You may also learn about publications, blogs, virtual communities, or other mediums the client uses to access information about the industry. Write these down as well. This is essential for several reasons. First, it will certainly help you learn more about your industry and the most

.

important issues facing your clients and prospects. It will also provide you potential 'content marketing' for generating meaningful interactions with both clients and prospects. What could be better than mailing an article or emailing a link or post to someone and saying, "I saw this and thought of you." This can be a great tool to touch a client or work to engage a prospect you are targeting. You can also use some of this information for your social media posts on LinkedIn. Creating meaningful content can be a time-consuming and difficult endeavor. Why not allow other experts to do this work for you? These activities will further demonstrate your credibility as a resource and show you are actively engaged in the industry.

What are your priorities for the balance of the year? Is there anything I can do to be of assistance to you?

This is a great question because you are asking to learn more about their priorities. What is important to them? In some cases, their priorities may have something to do with what you sell. Other times it may be related to an entirely different type of need. Either way there is a unique opportunity for you to assist the client on a personal level.

Let us say their priority for the year has to do with creating Individual Development Plans for their staff. While the Human Resources department has rolled out the plan, the client may still find it difficult to complete the task. Perhaps you know someone who has experience with employee development plans. Again, you do not have to leap up and immediately shout out the answer. But you could probe and ask if they would be interested in some assistance from an industry professional. If they say 'yes', you could say you may have an industry expert who could assist them and offer to make the introduction. You will earn bonus points for being a great resource and be on your way to earning the coveted trusted advisor status. Use your creativity to find unique ways to offer value to everyone you meet. They will remember your efforts and likely work to reward your generosity.

Competitive Accounts

You will also be working to initiate discussions with competitive accounts. Remember, your competitor's *client* list is your *prospect* list. An important part of sales success is generating business from new accounts, which essentially means stealing business from your competition. We will discuss this further, however, for now let us focus on the importance of using these contacts to learn more about your competitors and the industry overall. Essentially, you will be able to repackage the questions noted above for this very purpose. And you will want to have the chat with the prospect in very much the same way you did with your client. The main difference may be the prospect's willingness to divulge information. However, focus on obtaining help and not selling at this point. Remember, you asked this person if they would be willing to help you since you are new to the business. They agreed. So, stay the course and focus on learning. You will get to the selling later. And if you jump in and start selling too soon, you will have broken the deal which will not put you in the best light.

1. Why do you do business with your current supplier?
2. What do they do well? Is there anything they could do differently?
3. Who did you do business with before them? What, if anything, prompted you to switch providers?

4. How did you decide to select this company? What is the process your company uses for making these types of decisions?

5. What organizations do you belong to? How do you keep current on industry trends?

6. What are your priorities for the balance of the year? Is there anything I can do to be of assistance to you?

Please notice a few changes to the wording to each of the questions. Essentially you are looking to uncover the same information as when you were interviewing your clients, but how you ask a question is just as important as what you ask. Especially, "Is there anything they could do differently?" This is where you may uncover some pain points about their current relationship. But again, let us remember not to jump into a sales presentation even if you have the magic potion to solve their pain. Continue through the interview and collect all the information you can. You can end the conversation with a genuine 'thank you' and then suggest you talk again, as you may have some ideas for their consideration.

Teammates

Learning from teammates is another easy way to fast track your development. However, you should not simply choose the most friendly or approachable teammate for guidance. The goal is to learn, and you should focus your time and energy learning from the very best. While this might take more time initially, it will surely pay dividends in the long run. You may find everyone on your team is willing to share what they know. There is no reason not to learn from them as well. However, you want to find the high performers in each area of your business to observe and shadow. While many may be willing to offer advice and guidance worthy of consideration, you want to see how the superstars perform. They are the ones in the top 10% of ultra-high performers. They are the ones who are achieving the greatest results. They are the ones you want to model.

You should recognize that not everyone is a great teacher. Some people are very good at what they do but are not the best at sharing their skills effectively. However, if you are patient and are willing to dig a little, you will get to see firsthand what they are doing to make them the most successful members of your organization. You should not limit yourself to spending time with only high-performing sales professionals. You should also spend time with the most proficient people in every department that you will rely on to build your business. Depending on your company, this may include customer service, operations, finance, marketing, and the field service team.

It would be wise to ask your direct teammates and manager for their advice to identify the 'rock stars' of the organization. Who do people admire for their ability to do their jobs at the highest level? When you develop this list, visit each person and ask them for their assistance. It is as simple as introducing yourself and saying, "I understand that you are one of the best (title) in (department). Would you be willing to teach me about what you do?" I think you will find most people willing to spend some time with you. You will also start to cultivate important relationships with the key people in the organization, those with a reputation for getting things done. This will be helpful as you build your business.

During these learning sessions be sure to understand how their group or function fits into the overall organization. How do they spend their time? How do they interface with clients? What specific knowledge do they possess about your company's products and services that might be helpful to you in the future? How can you ensure you make their job and life easy? If you are meeting with someone in customer service, for example, they may tell you that they hate it when salespeople dump an order on their desk filled with errors. Ask them to teach you the proper way to complete an order package so they look forward to processing your orders first. These are the little things that add up to make a big difference in your future success. You want to make friends with the people who form the backbone of your organization so they will be willing to help you and make your life easier as well.

After meeting with each person, be sure to send them a handwritten thank-you card expressing your gratitude and appreciation. You may even want to include a token gift like a small box of candy or cookies. This will show them you really appreciated their time and will further strengthen your relationship. Be sure to stop in and chat them up when you are in the office or even consider treating them to lunch. Some of these people will form the core of your support team that we will discuss in Chapter 18.

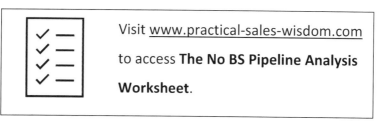

Visit www.practical-sales-wisdom.com to access **The No BS Pipeline Analysis Worksheet**.

Learning Points:

1. There is always something to learn so be a student and absorb as much information as possible each day. Sometimes you will learn a new best practice and sometimes you will learn what not to do. Either way, you are learning, and you need to make this a daily activity.

2. Clients and prospects have a wealth of information to offer if you are willing to ask for their help. People love to share their knowledge because it feeds their ego and makes them feel important. Welcome the opportunity

to have them tell you what you need to know to be successful.

3. When you are meeting with clients and prospects be sure to take notes and dig deep into each response to understand the underlying reasons for what they are telling you. If they tell you your product or service saves them time, ask them how it saves them time, and how much time it saves them. Quantify the responses so you can effectively use this information when talking with a potential prospect about the solutions you offer and specifically how it will benefit them.

4. If a client or prospect hints about a need they have during the interview, do not change course to engage them on it immediately. Complete the discussion to obtain the information you were working to collect initially and then ask them if you could schedule a follow up time to discuss their potential need (or dissatisfaction) in greater detail. They will appreciate you honoring your original commitment and will be more likely to schedule additional time with you.

5. Your teammates know the company and industry better than you. Take advantage of this knowledge by asking them for assistance. Be sure to demonstrate your gratitude for their help so you can develop a strong relationship which offer mutual benefits.

"The questions you ask are more important than the things you could ever say."

Thomas Freese

Section 2: The Sales Process

"Sell the problem you solve, not the product."

Unknown

Chapter 8: The Sales Process

It is essential to have a well-documented sales process you can use to guide your activities from initial engagement through conclusion. The company that has hired you should be able to provide this to you. If they have not provided it, ask your manager for a copy. If it is not something readily available, ask to review the components of the sales process with your manager. Be sure you can document the activities that describe the typical sales engagement from lead received through successful conclusion. Each sales cycle may be slightly different in practice but having a process will illuminate the way forward. You may find some differences between the sales process for different products or services you sell. That is fine. Just be sure to understand how each operates to ensure you can properly monetize your efforts.

Before we begin in earnest, I think it is important to disclose that having a process does not mean you will be following the steps without thought or consideration. In other words, a process will help you plan a general direction, but it will not determine every step you might need to take during your journey. In most cases a sales process is a general guide including known best practices which will ensure you do not miss an important step in the process. Again, while every situation is different, there are certainly enough similarities which will make this a useful tool. However, it is not intended to be a step-by-step guide that guarantees success each time.

It is also important to understand each prospect believes their situation is unique. They never want to hear they have a 'common' problem or issue that you can easily address. In their mind they are special and, therefore, their challenge is special. Even if you have seen this challenge a hundred times before, you never want to characterize it in those terms. Rather, it would be better to acknowledge the 'uniqueness' of their situation and exhibit confidence in your ability to help them as you have helped other clients in similar situations. For example, *"That is quite an interesting challenge. It reminds me of a few other situations which were similar in nature. Fortunately, we were able to assist those clients and I am confident we can assist you as well."* Prospects want to be assured you can help them and their business. As a matter of fact, a recent survey found that 77% of buyers want to work with sales professionals who can demonstrate deep insights into the buyer's business.[15] They have certain expectations of the value they want to see created in order to invest their time with you.

We will use the following diagram to denote the typical sales cycle. You should adapt this format as necessary to

---

[15] Forrester. (2016, Sept.). *How B2B Sellers Win In The Age Of The Customer: Evolved Selling Creates Lucrative And Loyal Relationships.* A Forrester Consulting Thought Leadership Paper Commissioned By Mediafly. Retrieved March 14, 2022 from https://ejjg6j4772uoghudr74bot9-wpengine.netdna-ssl.com/wp-content/uploads/2017/12/MediaflyEvolvedSellingWhitePaper.pdf

align with what you have been provided. However, the explanation for each step should still prove to be useful.

The Sales Process

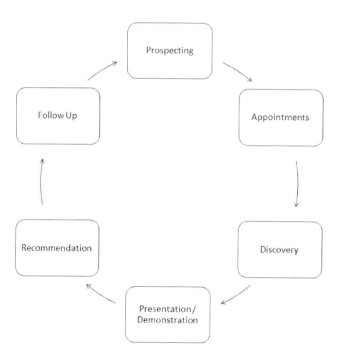

It is also important to understand there are three distinct processes going on simultaneously.[16] There is the sales process, the buying process, and the decision-making process. As you know, the sales process is the approach you take to engage the prospect to work the opportunity to conclusion. The buying process is the prospect's process and policies to identify their needs, evaluate their options, and, finally, make a decision. It is how they typically engage vendors to find solutions for their business. And finally, there is the decision-making process, which is how the particular people involved, the stakeholders, in the buying process will make a decision based on what is in their personal best interest. The buying process and decision-making process are both from the 'buyer' perspective, but these processes do not necessarily perfectly align. Remember, we are all motivated by our own self-interest: "what is best for me?" Do not attempt to change this viewpoint; it is ingrained in each of us. Rather, understand how this viewpoint motivates and directs behavior to manage and influence it effectively.

---

[16] Blount, J. (2017, Mar. 20). *Sales EQ: How Ultra High Performers Leverage Sales-Specific Emotional Intelligence to Close the Complex Deal*. Wiley. p. 137.

As an employee for a company, I may have the responsibility to purchase certain items. While my relationship to the company may dictate that I consider the best interests of the company primarily, do not think I will allow a decision to negatively impact me personally. If I will be using the product or service, or if it will directly impact me or my team, I will want my preferences represented in the selection process. To be honest, I may even want my preferences, to the degree the decision will impact my daily life, to supersede the company's interests. It is common for self-interest to drive more of the buying process than anything else despite claims to the contrary. We are far more emotional than we are logical. It is simply a fact of human nature.

I should add that there is a difference between a customer and a client. A customer is someone who has bought from you once. A client is someone who buys from you again and again. In the world of professional sales, we are interested in developing clients. It is clearly easier to get a client to buy again than it is to find someone completely new to buy from you for the first time. To develop clients, you will need to develop mutually-beneficial relationships. This is a relationship where you each benefit from the partnership according to your needs, desires, and priorities. You should look at every opportunity not simply as a chance to make a sale, but to secure a client. As Jeffrey Gitomer, the King of Sales, says, "If you make a sale, you can earn a commission. If you make a friend, you can earn a fortune."

During the discovery process, it is important to ask questions about the buying process as well to gain an understanding of what is most important to each stakeholder. A stakeholder is a person with an interest or concern in something. In this case, someone who is impacted by the product or service you offer. And while you will be asking questions, you never want to engage in an 'interrogation' session with the prospect. You want to have a conversation. As you increase your proficiency in asking good questions, actively listening to the responses, and then asking appropriate follow up questions, you will see how conversational the process becomes. This will make the person you are speaking with more comfortable which will encourage them to be more forthcoming and honest in the information they provide. You, in turn, will be more confident and professional, reinforcing the trust that is being developed between you and your prospect or client. It is a perpetual cycle that will grow stronger with time and practice.

You should never ask the person that you first meet with if they are the decision maker. This question can be seen as threatening to their ego or standing. Depending on what type of product or service you sell, and the potential impact to a larger part of the business, the more you will find several or many 'decision influencers.' The more impactful the decision is to the business, the greater the number of people and layers of management that may be involved. Rather, it is preferred to ask, "How does your company generally make a decision on a project like this?" They may then tell you they have the authority to make the decision, or they may disclose their supervisor, or a committee of stakeholders, is responsible for the final determination. You should work to identify specifically who those people are so you can understand what motivates them and how you can influence a decision in your favor.

While you can certainly ask outright for the names of the people involved, you may find your point of contact unwilling to divulge that information early in the process or before you have had a chance to build a trusting relationship. However, it is early in the process when you need this information to best position yourself for a win. Instead, use questions to uncover this information. For example, consider asking, "Could you tell me a little about your goals and objectives for the project?" You can then follow up that question by asking, "Could you now share with me what the other stakeholders consider to be important?" In this way, you are giving the prospect the opportunity to share his views as well as provide insight to the other stakeholders' interests and priorities. You should also consider while each of these stakeholders plays a role in the decision-making process, none may independently have the authority to say 'yes'. However, each may have the power to say 'no'. Depending on their level of influence, the 'no' may become a final 'no'.

Using some careful questioning techniques, you should be able to uncover details about each of the stakeholders involved. For example, when you ask the question noted above, the prospect might say, "George is concerned about how this new system might impact our network." You can follow up by asking, "That's interesting. Why is George concerned about this?" The prospect might reply, "As our CIO he is responsible for..." Now you have obtained a name and title of one of the stakeholders involved. You may follow up by asking, "You said there is someone else on the committee who expressed a concern about training, could you tell me more?" The prospect might respond, "Mary generally ends up owning many of our new systems and she hates to be the one to train everyone in the department." You can then respond with, "Sounds like this has happened to Mary in the past, could you tell me how this might impact her day-to-day responsibilities?" To which the prospect responds, "She is our Chief Administrator with many other priorities..." Now you have a second name and title. This simple process will allow you to gather the names and titles of the stakeholders and begin to understand how they will each play a role in the evaluation and decision-making process.

The goal is to have a talk. To chat. To engage in a casual, but meaningful, conversation where you ask thoughtful questions, the prospect provides important information, and you continue to probe until you solicit all the information required to gain a complete understanding of their situation. Probing is a questioning technique that requires you to keep digging for information. You ask a question and receive a response. However, you don't accept the answer until you ask some follow-up questions to really understand the context of the answer and how it fits in to the overall discussion. Keep digging until you hit bedrock. Notice I used the word 'understanding'. This goes beyond just 'listening' to a deeper state in which you truly gain insight and perspective. This has a dual effect. First, it demonstrates your willingness to listen to gain understanding. The prospect will appreciate your attentiveness and genuine interest. Second, it will allow you to uncover the real issues, what is vital, and how those involved in the process can be motivated to decide in your favor. It is essential to get into the weeds and uncover the real motivations and priorities for each stakeholder. You want to learn how this decision may impact them personally as well as professionally. Everyone is motivated by their own interests. Be sure you understand how you can motivate them to select your offering.

Empathy

A key part of gaining and communicating understanding is empathy. Empathy is the ability to connect with someone on a very personal level and understand how they are feeling in a certain situation. It is a key skill to develop and master since it goes beyond hearing the facts of the situation to understanding the impact the prospect experienced, often at a personal level. By understanding the emotional side, you can further strengthen your connection by acknowledging their emotions. For example, your prospect may tell you her current device fails often, adding, "It drives me crazy!" While you want to note frequent breakdowns as a potential problem to address, the fact the device drives her crazy is more important. You could reply, "I am sorry to hear that. How does this impact you personally?" Here you demonstrate you are listening to how she feels as much as you are listening to what she says. She may respond by telling you the breakdowns means she has to miss lunch or work longer hours. Now, you are really getting to the implications of frequent breakdowns and the personal impact on her. You would be wise to reply, "I understand how you feel. I have been in a similar situation and can appreciate the frustration this must cause for you missing lunch or arriving home late. I may be able to help you, as I have helped other people, who faced a similar challenge. Would you be open to discussing this?" Again, your statement demonstrates you are listening to her reasoning as much as you are understanding her emotions. This, in turn, should strengthen your ability to build a true connection. More than anything else, people want to be listened to and understood.[17] In the end emotion drives action, not logic.

I firmly believe that our prospects will tell us everything we need to know if we just ask great questions and actively listen. I say 'actively' listen to denote a true skill which goes beyond just hearing the words or waiting for your turn to speak. Active listening is hard work, requiring

---

[17] Staley, L. (2018, May 21). *Most People Want to be Seen, Heard, and Understood: Listening as a Lifelong Practice*. LinkedIn. Retrieved from https://www.linkedin.com/pulse/most-people-want-seen-heard-understood-listening-lifelong-staley/

concentration to understand what is being said as well as what is not being said. The power of great questions is to continue to mine for information from the prospect to get all the details possible. Further, it allows you to uncover the emotional drivers that will influence, if not determine, how the decision will really be made. People are more emotional than they are rational. You must look for the answer as well as the corresponding feeling (emotion) to ensure they are aligned. Done properly the process will assist the prospect in gaining clarity about their own situation. They may finally be thinking and feeling in terms which previously they were unaware. As a result, they may conclude on their own your product or service is exactly what they need to solve their problem. Instead of convincing, you simply help guide the prospect through their own discovery to reach a decision.

Great Questions

As you learn your business and industry, be sure to develop a list of powerful questions to ask during the sales process. I have found it useful to create a list that I can refer to as needed. You may even observe others asking great questions and you will be able to learn from them as well.

The other benefit to having a list is you will be able to actively listen to your prospect or client instead of trying to think of the next question to ask when they are speaking. Having questions at the ready will allow you to be engaged and appropriately prepared to have a meaningful conversation. Remember you are not questioning like it is an interrogation. Rather, you are engaged in a conversation which promotes a willingness to share factual information. This information will help you understand and best position yourself to win the business.

Learning Points:

1. A sales process is a guide to the interaction you will have with a typical prospect. It is not guaranteed that you will follow each step in order, but it should be seen as a guide to help you structure your engagement to give yourself the best opportunity to win the business. You should review and update your sales process on a regular basis to incorporate what you have learned, and leverage discovered best practices.

2. Recognize the prospect has both a buying process as well as a decision-making process that are operating while you are following your sales process. Be aware of where you are in each cycle to ensure you respond to needs and concerns in a timely manner.

3. You steer the conversation by asking thoughtful questions. The person asking the questions is in control and directs the conversation. Learn to have great conversations with prospects and clients and listen carefully to what they say. Most likely, they will tell you all you need to know to understand their needs and their objectives, to earn their business.

4. Empathy is a key ingredient in developing a strong connection with prospects and clients. It demonstrates your ability to understand on a personal level and will strengthen your ability to connect with them.

5. Develop a list of great questions to have available so you can actively listen while being prepared to lead a productive conversation. Rehearse and role play using your questions to fine tune your approach to ensure you are putting forth your best effort.

"How you sell matters. What your process is matters. But how your customers feel when they engage with you matters more."

Tiffani Bova

"Great salespeople are relationship builders who provide value and help their customers win."

Jeffrey Gitomer

Chapter 9: Appointments

For sales professionals, face-to-face appointments with prospects and clients is one of the most important activities. In most cases, this is where the real selling is done. In the past, these were conducted in person, however, with the advent of improved technology and recent health concerns, a substantial amount of face-to-face selling is now done online. In either environment, the need to generate a suitable number of appointments will be critical to your success. This chapter will provide a brief description of the different ways to accomplish this goal and some common best practices. You need to remember why the prospect agreed to the meeting in the first place. They are expecting that you are a well-prepared expert who will educate them, provide thought leadership, and offer new insights to solve their problems.[18]

Meeting Preparation

It is imperative that you invest the time to prepare for every meeting. I know, most salespeople 'wing it'. Yes, they do. However, I think we already agreed that you want to become an ultra-high performing sales professional, right? In that case, you want to be 'fanatical' about preparing for every meeting to ensure you demonstrate your professionalism and keep each opportunity on a sure and steady path to success. This is especially true for a first or initial appointment with a new prospect. You want to convey confidence to ensure you earn the right to obtain the next appointment. Among the key areas to research in order to be prepared[19]:

- Company Research – This includes using a tool like Dun & Bradstreet to run a credit report and discover

---

[18] Samoisette, M. (2018, Nov. 5). *Sales Processified: How Small Business CEOs Can Implement a Sales Process That Gets Results*. Elevate Coaching Press.
[19] Asher, J. (2021, June). Presentation.

information about the size and scope of operations. Are they financially sound? Are they growing, shrinking, or stagnate? Take time to review their website for recent announcements, their mission statement and core values, their leadership team, and anything else that might relate to the solutions you provide. Who are their main competitors? What is going on in their industry that may influence their future behavior? If they are a publicly-traded company, go to the U.S. Securities and Exchange Commission website at www.sec.gov and review recent filings. There is a wealth of information about companies in these documents.

- Buyer or Point-of-Contact Research – Use social media, like LinkedIn, and search tools, like Google, to research the person or people you will be meeting. What insights can you gain about them? There are tools, like Crystal Knows, that will provide guidance about a person's personality type based on the information they have posted in their LinkedIn profile. Learning about someone's personality traits before you meet with them will let you prepare and do your best to modify your style to align with their personality more closely. This has been referred to as 'mirroring' since your behavior reflects their behavior to a certain degree.[20] Mirroring needs to be done in a subtle manner to avoid it being artificial and noticeable. Where it can assist is in helping you understand if the person is directive (gets down to business quick) or more social, for example. The directive personality may not appreciate small talk while the social person would enjoy your efforts to build a better rapport.

The type of information that is most important will depend on what you sell. However, basic information about the company and the key contacts is essential to demonstrate your level of preparation. Being able to ask about a recent acquisition or change in leadership will demonstrate your professionalism and business acumen.

---

[20] Thompson, J. (2012, Sept. 9). *Mimicry and Mirroring Can Be Good or Bad*. Psychology Today. Retrieved from https://www.psychologytoday.com/ca/blog/beyond-words/201209/mimicry-and-mirroring-can-be-good-or-bad

Visit www.practical-sales-wisdom.com to access the **Company Research Worksheet**.

Company-Scheduled Appointments

Perhaps you are fortunate enough to have your company schedule some or all your appointments utilizing a combination of outbound telemarketing and lead generation advertising efforts. There should certainly be a defined process for how these leads are distributed and scheduled. In some cases, you may be provided leads that require you to contact the prospect to schedule the appointment.

If your company is placing appointments on your calendar, you will want to make sure your calendar is always up to date. Further, you will want to work to ensure that new appointments are put near each other with still sufficient time to conduct each meeting and travel to the next appointment. This is one of the advantages of virtual meetings, the commuting time is dramatically shortened, and you can schedule more meetings each day.

If you are provided leads that require you to schedule the appointment, you must treat this as a priority activity. If someone has either called in or submitted an online request for information, you will want to contact this person immediately, for several reasons:

1. They are interested now. They just called or submitted a lead form through your website or responded to a digital advertisement. What you offer or sell is currently top of mind for this prospect.

2. They may be contacting other vendors offering similar products and the first one to return their call will secure the coveted appointment. When someone is in the 'buying' mode, they want immediate attention. Even if the prospect will meet with several providers, the first company through the door has a distinct advantage. As a result, they can influence the buying

criteria and evaluation process by elevating their position and making it more difficult for other vendors to compete on equal footing.

3. You want to show them they are important and worthy of your immediate attention. We all want to feel special. Would a prospect feel important submitting an information request and then receiving a call within minutes? Special indeed.

Helpful Appointment Setting and Confirmation Tips

Tip 1: So I am Properly Prepared

If your appointments are set by your company on your calendar, you will still want to call and confirm these meetings in advance. One of the strategies that has worked well is to place a call as follows:

You: "Hello Mr. Prospect, this is (Your Name) from (Your Company). Is this a good time for you to speak with me?"

Prospect: "Certainly."

You: "Thank you. I wanted to confirm our upcoming appointment on (Day and Time). **So that I am properly prepared for our meeting**, could you please provide me a quick overview of your (project/need/issue/problem)?"

Prospect: "Absolutely." (Provides some details).

You: "Great. In addition, do you have **any special concerns** that I should be aware of about this project?"

Prospect: "Yes, I'm concerned about XYZ."

You: "Thank you for providing me this information. I will send you a **confirmation email with an agenda** outlining the items we discussed today. Please let me know if you require any assistance prior to our meeting on (Date/Time). Thank you again and have a great day."

Let us review some of the key points that are in bold above. The phrase, **"So that I am properly prepared for our meeting"** coupled with **"any special concerns"** demonstrates your interest in respecting the prospect's time as well as your own time. It says, "I am a professional and will invest time prior to our meeting to understand your needs, develop some ideas, and be prepared to provide you the best possible buying experience."

The sending of a **"confirmation email with an agenda"** is further proof that you value their time, and you are a consummate professional. You can use a template to generate these emails efficiently with only some minor personalization based on each discussion. However, let me ask you this, how many other salespeople, in any industry, are sending this type of confirmation? Very few, if any. Probably only the top performers. This is another easy way to differentiate yourself.

Tip 2: Email Confirmation and Agenda

You can either send a separate email for the agenda or attach it to the calendar invitation you send the prospect/client confirming your appointment. If the appointment was scheduled for you by your company, a separate email makes sense, but if you are scheduling the appointment yourself, you can save time by making it an attachment to the calendar invitation.

The confirmation can be brief and based on a template you utilize repeatedly to save time. It will also ensure that you include all the key points in every communication. This way you are effective and efficient. In the email you will provide a very short review of the purpose of the meeting and highlight the prospect's key objective. You would have gathered this information from the pre-appointment call you made earlier. Next, you outline a very basic agenda. As you will notice, the agenda aligns with the Opening Statement you will make when you arrive and sit down with the prospect. What is most important about this process is setting expectations and communicating your respect for their time (and yours). It will also demonstrate your listening ability and your desire to understand. Yes, when you state in the email the purpose of the meeting (their needs) and their desired outcome (goal), you show that you listened to them carefully and made notes of what was said. This is impactful. This simple act will help differentiate you from not only your competitors, but from every other salesperson out there.

Here is an example of a confirmation email sent separately:

To: Prospect

From: Sales Professional

Subject: Appointment Confirmation – Tuesday, May 2nd at 1:00 PM

Dear Ms. Prospect,

Thank you for taking a few minutes to speak with me on the phone earlier today. To confirm, we will be discussing your need to (upgrade your system, add a capability, change a service). Your primary objective is to (save time, save money, become more efficient).

Here is a brief agenda we can use to maximize our time together:

1. Introductions
2. Review Your Current Situation
3. Discuss Your Goals and Objectives
4. Review Potential Options
5. Determine Next Steps

If there is anything you would like to add to the agenda, please let me know. I look forward to seeing you on Tuesday, May 2nd at 1:00 PM at your office.

If you need to speak with sooner, please contact me at XXX-XXX-XXXX. Thank you.

Regards,

Sales Professional

When I first required my sales team to send these communications, I know they were a little hesitant. They initially viewed it as extra work without an obvious benefit. However, they soon discovered the power of this simple activity. They started receiving emails back from their prospects thanking them and acknowledging their professionalism. While not everyone responded, many did, and they unequivocally noted their appreciation. The prospect appreciated working with someone who was organized, prepared, and ready to assist them. Guess what? The prospect appreciated the email and it set the stage for building a successful relationship. Afterwards, it became a normal part of what the team did to differentiate ourselves from everyone else.

Tip 3: Meeting Follow-Up Communication

A great strategy is to follow up a meeting with a thank you email which includes the main points discussed and the action items to which both parties committed. While the task is simple and will only take a few moments to prepare, it sends a powerful message to your prospect or client. It demonstrates you were listening and taking notes to ensure appropriate follow up on what was discussed. More than anything, people want to be listened to and understood. They appreciate those sales professionals who demonstrate this quality and are more likely to want to do business with them in the future. Here is an example of a follow up email:

To: Prospect

From: Sales Professional

Subject: Meeting Notes and Action Items

Dear Ms. Prospect,

Thank you again for taking the time to meet with me today. I enjoyed our conversation and appreciated you sharing with me details about your business and upcoming requirements.

- You have an XYZ coming to the end of the lease which you will want to upgrade.
- Your requirements include:
  - Item 1
  - Item 2
  - Item 3
- It is most important to you the new system do ...

You committed to speaking with your team to determine who should attend the upcoming demonstration at our office. I committed to reviewing the schedule and providing you a few dates and time for consideration.

If there is anything else, please let me know. Thank you again for your time and consideration. I look forward to our upcoming meeting.

Regards,

Sales Professional

Ask yourself this question: how many sales professionals take the time to send this type of communication to a prospect or client after a meeting? Very few. Yet, as you can see, it clearly delineates the topics discussed and the upcoming commitments each party made during the meeting. This email is also an easy way to help the prospect loop in other members of their team to determine who will be attending the proposed demonstration. You have done the hard work for them which makes it easier for them to follow through on their commitment. And, by using the template feature available in most email tools, creating these personalized emails will be quick and easy. This is exactly the type of communication which will demonstrate your professionalism.

Tip 4: Has Anything Changed?

This is a fantastic question to ask your contact each time you have a conversation. As you start the discussion simply ask, "Has anything changed since we last spoke?" In some cases, nothing has changed. Other times you will learn of new requirements, or a new stakeholder becoming involved, or even a new competitor who is now being seriously considered. Give yourself the opportunity to get up to speed on what has transpired since your last interaction by asking for an update. Another great question to ask at the start of a meeting is, "Is there anything else you want to be sure we cover during our meeting?"[21] Again, these questions validate if anything has changed or if there are other issues the prospect or client wants to discuss.

 Visit www.practical-sales-wisdom.com to access the **Executive Meeting Checklist**.

Is Cold Calling Effective?

There has been an ongoing debate in sales regarding the effectiveness of cold calling. Cold calling, by definition, is proactively contacting a prospect who you do not know, for the purpose of determining if they are interested in your product or service. This may be done through in-person

---

[21] Blount, J. (2019, Jan. 1). *Objections: The Ultimate Guide for Mastering the Art and Science of Getting Past NO*. Wiley.

visits, phone calls, email, direct mail, or social media. To be fair, it is likely one of the least effective methods of engagement. However, when you are new to sales and have not yet developed enough contacts and clients, you will often find it necessary to undertake this activity to make new connections and uncover opportunities.

I like to think of prospecting in terms of a waterfall. At the top you have a personal referral, someone who knows or does business with you who then recommends you to a colleague who has an immediate need for the product or service you offer. This is the best opportunity to develop a new relationship and make a sale. Then, you move down to a warm introduction which may develop into a potential engagement. Next you have various lead sources where a prospect self-identifies as having an interest, but you do not have a personal connection to them. And finally, at the bottom, you have proactive cold calling. Reaching out to people who you do not know but you suspect may have a need, based on the characteristics of their business alone.

We would all like to spend our time at the top of the

waterfall, receiving those personal referrals from people wanting to buy. But in the beginning, this is a difficult task. Your network of connections isn't developed sufficiently to provide enough referrals to generate the opportunities and revenue required to achieve success. However, over time, your network will certainly improve and increase. In the interim, you will have to work the rest of the waterfall to generate enough new opportunities. There are some great resources for helping you increase your effectiveness in this area.

Meeting Opening Statement

As much as your prospect is evaluating a working relationship with you, you should also be evaluating a working relationship with the prospect. Try out this opening statement:

Prospect, thank you for meeting with me today. What I would like to do, if it is alright with you, is to better understand your situation, requirements, and goals. Then, I will tell you a little about how I think I may be able to help you. Then, based on that discussion, we can determine if it makes sense to work together and determine the next logical steps. How does that sound to you?

Let's be sure to understand what makes this opening so powerful. First, you are suggesting how the conversation should proceed and asking for the prospect's agreement. You are deferring to their authority by posing the question this way. Next, you are asking them to speak first, so you can better understand their situation and challenges. After hearing about what issues are most important to them, you will then offer some suggestions for their consideration. This is the "How I may be able to help you" part of the discussion.

Now, the next part is very important because it is the disruptor. A disruptor is something that contradicts a bias, in such a way as to draw immediate attention to the discrepancy.[22] The person disrupted will immediately try to

---

[22] Howard, C. (2013, Mar. 27). *Disruption Vs. Innovation: What's The Difference?* Forbes. Retrieved from https://www.forbes.com/sites/carolinehoward/2013/03/27/you-say-innovator-i-say-disruptor-whats-the-difference/?sh=499248626f43

understand what has occurred and pay greater attention as a result. "From there we can decide together if it makes sense for our companies to work together." In terms of sales psychology, this phrase will awaken the prospect's subconscious to scream out, "What do you mean? YOU may NOT want to sell ME something?" You see, we are conditioned to believe that salespeople always want to sell us something whether it is in our best interest or not. But you come in and question that assumption (bias, if you will), by saying you and the prospect may not be a good fit to work together. This will differentiate you from every other salesperson. It will cause the prospect's brain to want to pay attention in order to understand why this might be the case, since it violates a fundamental bias they hold generally about all salespeople.[23] Jeb Blount covers impactful opening statements in more detail in his book entitled *Sales EQ*; I highly recommend you read this book.

---

[23] Blount, J. (2017, Mar. 20). *Sales EQ: How Ultra High Performers Leverage Sales-Specific Emotional Intelligence to Close the Complex Deal.* Wiley.

Sitting Down with A Prospect or Client

Here is a quick note on the best method for sitting down with a prospect or client for a face-to-face meeting. When possible, avoid sitting directly across a table or desk from them. This position is adversarial by nature. The desk or table creates a barrier. This is not an ideal environment for building a connection and eventually a mutually-beneficial relationship. Instead, try sitting at a 45-degree angle to the person you are meeting with, to make it less adversarial and more complementary. As a matter of fact, if you are meeting with more than one person, work to position yourself at the head of the table so you can have one person on each side of you on an angle. Take every precaution to not sit directly across the table from your prospect, as if you are engaged in some high-powered negotiation. Create a positive 'we' environment, not a 'you' versus 'me' environment.

Requesting Strategic Introductions

One area which is probably underutilized is the art of asking for a strategic introduction. The prevalence of social media platforms, like LinkedIn, make learning about potential connections easier than ever before. You should be sure to develop a professional online profile. Further, you should invest time each day to build your personal brand by sharing content, commenting on other posts, and growing your network of connections. This is a critical way to have potential connections, partners, and prospects find and connect with you.

We understand the value inherent in a referral. When someone recommends us to a colleague or friend, they are essentially saying, "I trust this person and you should too. They can help you." This is one of the greatest compliments any professional can receive. Plus 84% of business-to-business (B2B) buyers most value a referral from someone they trust.[24] However, as discussed, developing enough referrals early in your sales career can be a challenge. The first step is to ask for introductions or referrals once you have secured a new client. Remember, the people you are selling to often know more people like themselves. These

[24] Larrison, A. (2021, Jan. 10). *15 surprising referral marketing statistics that you must know*. Okiano. Retrieved March 14, 2022 from https://www.okianomarketing.com/15-surprising-referral-marketing-statistics-that-you-must-know/

are the types of people you want to know. As Alan Weiss says, "Referrals are the 'coinage of my realm' in this business, and I'm going to work very hard to maximize your project's outcomes so that you'll be very comfortable is providing these at the right point.". Absolutely true!

However, there is a better way to solicit proactive introductions. If you have a new or existing client who you have been working with, it is entirely appropriate to ask them for a referral. Most sales professionals would say something to the effect of, "I really appreciate your business. Do you happen to know of anyone else who might benefit from our products or services?" I am sure some clients can offer a suggestion or two, but I feel as if this puts the client on the spot. How would you respond to a similar question after you made a significant purchase or investment? As much as you might want to provide a referral, I think you might find it equally difficult to come up with a name. You would probably end up saying something like, "Not at this moment, but if I run into anyone with a similar need, I'll be sure to recommend you." While this is nice, it does little to generate a potential lead right now.

Here is the advantage offered by technologies such as LinkedIn. If you are not already connected to your clients and key prospects, you should send a personal note to connect with them today. Now you will have access to their connections. A little effort on your part will offer you the opportunity to request and receive meaningful introductions. You can review a client's list of known associates and find two or three which appear to align with your ideal prospect profile. Instead of asking for a generic referral, you can ask for a warm strategic introduction. For example:

You: "Mrs. Client, thank you again for selecting me and my company to be your partner. We appreciate your business. I was wondering if I could request a favor?"

Client: "Certainly."

You: "My best new clients come from referrals from people like you. I noticed on LinkedIn you are connected to Mr. Prospect and Mrs. Prospect. Do you know them well?"

Client: "Yes, I have known them both for many years. We are members of an industry group."

You: "Very nice. I was wondering if you would be willing to introduce me. They work for companies which may have a need for the services I offer. Would you be willing to help me?"

Client: "Absolutely. How can I assist you?"

You: "I will send you an email with my contact information and a brief description of the services we have provided to you. Then, if you could simply forward the message to each person, copying me, it will open the door to a conversation. How does that sound?"

Client: "I would be happy to do that for you."

You: "Thank you."

This approach requires you to do the heavy lifting. You will need to do some research to find the most strategic connections to request a warm introduction. Remember, people do business with you, in part because they like you. Most of them would be happy to help you. And the easier you make it for them to help you, the more likely they are to help you build your business. And this approach does not eliminate the chance your client will say, "While those are two great people to meet, I know someone else you should speak with as well."

Imagine how many potential introductions are waiting for you right now? If you are managing 25 client accounts, and could get two strategic introductions from each, you could be talking to an additional 50 potential prospects. How long and how much energy would it take you to generate this many new contacts by cold calling? Even if you could do it in the same amount of time, which I seriously doubt, you would be dealing with someone 'cold' versus a 'warm' introduction from a mutual business associate. The very act of making the introduction by your current client is a demonstration of the trust they have in you. This is powerful as the 'trust' is transferred from your client to a new potential contact.

Here is an example email requesting a strategic introduction:

To: Mrs. Client

From: Sales Professional

Subject: Introduction to Mr. Prospect

Dear Mrs. Client,

Thank you again for your time last week. I appreciate your willingness to introduce me to Mr. Prospect. Given the similarity of your businesses, it occurred to me Mr. Prospect may have an interest in our offerings, especially given your satisfaction in working with me and my company.

My contact information is listed below. I look forward to speaking with Mr. Prospect. Thank you again for making this introduction.

Regards,

Sales Professional

I would also recommend you not ask for too many introductions at one time from a single client. Requesting one or two at a time is polite. If they are the type of person who is connected to many potential prospects, you may want to spread out your requests over time. Be sure to send a handwritten note of thanks after each introduction. Again, a small token gift may be appropriate. If an introduction leads to a new client, be sure to thank them again and perhaps invite them to lunch to celebrate. There you can express your gratitude and perhaps solicit some additional assistance given their 'golden touch' for making quality introductions.

You should also consider providing your clients with leads, referrals, and strategic introductions. You may find these connections by reviewing your list of connections or by soliciting input from members of your lead group. You can ask your client if they are looking for assistance with gaining access to any specific people or companies. Perhaps you, a member of your team, or other professional colleague, has an established relationship and would be willing to arrange an introduction. By connecting people, you will make it easier to ask for and receive additional introductions yourself. Further, you will demonstrate the value you create for that client on a personal level and be on your way to establishing a trusted advisor status.

Expand Your Share of Wallet

It is always an interesting exercise to see exactly what a client is spending with you in comparison to what they are spending overall for all the products and services you offer. For example, if you sell a specific product and your client buys this only from you for $10,000 per year, you may think that you have 100% market share. Well, in that category, with that specific client, this might be true. But let's suppose the same client purchases other products you sell, but they buy these products from other providers. Let's suppose now the client spends $100,000 in total each year on products or services you offer. You went from 100% to 10% market share (or share of wallet) quickly. However, you can now realize the true potential of this relationship. There is more opportunity perhaps than you first considered. By developing an action plan, you will be able to investigate how you can create more value for your client, by purchasing what they are already buying, from you.

It is always easier to sell more to an existing client than it is to find a completely new client. While new clients are essential, you need to make sure you are maximizing the relationship with your current clients. Make sure you are earning as much of their 'wallet' (spending) as you can. Be sure to investigate their needs in other categories and uncover ways you can create additional value to capture that spend. This is a simple way to improve your relationship, protect your client base, and grow your business.

 Visit www.practical-sales-wisdom.com to access the **Share of Wallet Calculator**.

Learning Points:

1. You are not competing with just your industry competitors, but with all salespeople who are looking to gain the attention of decision influencers and decision makers. Be sure that you stand out from the crowd by doing the little things that demonstrate you are different and worthy of their time.

2. Making confirmation calls provides another touch point in building a relationship with a prospect. Take advantage of the opportunity to differentiate yourself by getting some background information so you will be properly prepared.

3. Send a confirmation email to show you were carefully listening and provide an agenda for the upcoming meeting. You will demonstrate your respect for their time and differentiate yourself as a professional who is ready to help them solve their business challenges.

4. Develop your meeting opening statement and be prepared to immediately differentiate yourself. Disrupt the inherent bias the prospect has about salespeople and get them focused on listening to what you have to offer and the value you can create for them.

5. Be sure to consistently request referrals and strategic introductions. It is among the easiest way to expand your circle of connections and start speaking to more potential prospects today.

6. Understand the big picture of spending your client is doing with all possible vendors for the products and services you offer. Be sure you are investing time expanding the relationship to capture as much of the business as possible.

"Small deeds done are better than great deeds planned."

Peter Marshall

"Approach each customer with the idea of helping him or her solve a problem or achieving a goal, not selling a product or service."

Brian Tracy

Chapter 10: The Discovery Process

The discovery process, or qualification process, in my opinion, is the most important part of the entire sales process. Discovery is the process of understanding and gaining insight into your prospect or client's business.[25] It may also be the least understood and mastered part of the sales process. This is where the rubber meets the road. I highly encourage you to become fluent in the proper approach to qualify each opportunity, determining if it is worth your best efforts to pursue and win the business. If, after speaking with the prospect, you discover they are not a good match for the value you create, or they are not the type of person you feel comfortable doing business with,

---

[25] Anderson, S. & Stein, D. (2016, April 4). Beyond the Sales Process: 12 Proven Strategies for a Customer-Driven World. AMACOM.

then run away. Don't walk, run! There is nothing worse than winning business which will cost you more time and money than either you or your company generated securing the business in the first place. Not everyone is a great prospect for what you have to offer. Be selective. Let your competitors have the other ones.

Discovery is where you should learn all about your prospect's business problems and how these problems impact them and their business, so that you can determine if you have a viable solution that can help them. It is also where you will learn how decisions about your product or service are made by the company and what you will have to do to justify a call to action. This is where you learn what you will need to do to eventually win the business. And like the other parts of the sales process, you do not want to take short cuts here. This is where you make your living and become a true high-performing sales professional.

Unfortunately, this is also where most sales professionals struggle. They are in such a rush to recommend a solution;

they scare the fish away from the hook. You must be patient and comprehensive in your approach. Discovery done properly makes the rest of the sales process much easier and will improve your ability to close more business. You will be really helping people solve a problem or helping them grow their business. This is also where preparation is key. As we discussed earlier, when you are preparing for an initial appointment, you need to do your homework and research the company to ensure you understand their business, industry, competitive pressures, and their clients. You want to position yourself as a businessperson capable of solving their most pressing business challenges.

I was recently speaking with some sales professionals who felt that closing was the most important skill. While I will concede you need to be able to ask for the business, when you have earned that privilege, most sales professional who have trouble closing business have really failed to conduct a thorough discovery. In an ideal sales cycle, as you go through each phase of the process it becomes logical, and almost obvious, to the prospect that your solution will help them and that they should buy from you. In some cases, they are asking you, "Where do I sign?" Remember what Jeffrey Gitomer says, "People don't like to be sold, but they love to buy." It is your job to help them buy from you the first time, then again and again. Proper discovery is what helps you make this a reality.

The discovery process will vary for different products and services. In some cases, you will only have to interface with a single person who has the authority to select the best offering and buy quickly. In other cases, you will have to interface with various decision influencers in a long and complex process. In other cases, you will have to collaborate with an entire committee of stakeholders. The number of influencers and the buying process will often be based on the impact your product or service will have on their business. If it has a small impact, fewer people may be involved. If it has a significant or enterprise-level impact, more people will typically be involved. In any event, you will have to identify what they want to accomplish (the problem they want to solve or the gain they want to achieve) and the best way to facilitate this exploration is with questions. Good questions are a sales professional's best friend. A solid questioning approach is the best way to really learn about the prospect, their problems, challenges, and frustrations. Great questions will open the way for you to really understand their business and how your product or solution can help them. And helping people is the essence of selling.

Implicit versus Explicit Needs

It is important to understand the difference between implicit needs and explicit needs. Briefly stated, an implicit need is something you believe the prospect desires (a capability or end state), while an explicit need is a stated need or objective by the prospect. The difference is that you will often recognize some implicit needs, but they are not as important as explicit needs. An explicit need is something stated by the prospect. They recognize the need and express it in terms of a 'must have' requirement. You will want to use the discovery process to bring explicit needs to the forefront as these needs will eventually form the basis for evaluating options and determining a course of action.

I am particularly fond of the book *SPIN Selling* by Neil Rackham and have been using his questioning techniques for over 25 years. It is the first book I assign to new sales professionals to read, and it is a skill set I help them develop through coaching very early in their career. The ability to ask thoughtful and appropriate questions is one of the keys to sales success. Essentially, there are four basic types of questions, and each has a distinct purpose. The four types of questions are situation, problem, implication, and need payoff. I will provide a brief overview to facilitate an explanation of the discovery process, however, this overview is not intended to teach you the proper use of these techniques. I highly recommend you read the book to fully learn the proper techniques.

Situation questions are designed to gather facts. Think in terms of "how many" or "how often" types of questions. These questions, by nature, are often closed-ended questions. While not always preferred, these questions are necessary to gather the initial facts to help you develop more thoughtful open-ended questions. Problem questions explore the issues and pain points the prospect is experiencing in their current situation. They are typically open-ended questions which allow the prospect to elaborate and share more information. These questions help define the problems they want to resolve, the pain they are experiencing. Examples include, "Tell me what challenges you have with your current unit?" or "How could your current system be improved?" However, it is the next type of question, the implication question, which is most critical. Implication questions uncover how the problem is impacting them and their business. This information is what you are really looking to ascertain during the discovery process. These questions are truly powerful because they will uncover those issues impacting the business and what could motivate them to change and buy from you.

For example, your prospect may be experiencing a problem with a printer which breaks down often. While it is inconvenient and frustrating, they may not be initially motivated to replace the printer with a new device. Perhaps it is in the budget for next year, but they don't have any funds available today. However, understanding how this unreliable printer impacts their business is the critical piece of information. If the prospect tells you their fulfillment department uses the printer to create the shipping labels so incoming orders can be sent to their clients, then what they are really saying is, "When the printer isn't working properly our entire business comes to a halt." That is what you really want to understand. This is exactly the type of problem that needs to be solved right now because of the significant impact it has on their business now.

Business Problems and Their Real Impact

Every business has problems. And not all problems are created equally. There are some problems, as inconvenient as they may be, that are just not worth the effort to solve. While the person experiencing this problem would like it to go away, there may be insufficient justification to act or make the required investment to eliminate the problem. Now, the beauty of implication questions is they uncover how a problem negatively impacts a business. These are the types of issues that impair, harm, or damage a business and impede it from achieving its goals and objectives. These issues can often negatively impact either the ability to generate revenue or facilitate a positive customer experience. These are exactly the types of issues that senior management wants to know about, address, and resolve. These are the problems that must be solved for a company to be successful and maintain a competitive advantage. Your ability to uncover these issues and understand how they impact a company, is what you will need to build a compelling case for the C-suite to act now. If your product can solve a real business issue and create a meaningful return on investment in short order, you may find that the funding for the expenditure is readily available. This is because the expenditure is no longer a "nice to have" but a "must have."

Let us go back to our example of the printer used to create shipping labels. If this device is unreliable and shipping labels cannot be printed when needed, what happens? Orders back up. Client shipments are delayed. This impacts revenue generation (payments) which will also impact the firm's profitability. If their clients experience consistent delays in their orders being fulfilled, they may decide to investigate other suppliers who are more dependable. Your prospect does not have a printer problem, they have a client experience and client retention problem. While the president of this company may not want to know about a faulty printer, he will certainly want to know about an issue that is causing his clients frustration and motivating them to explore alternatives and take their business elsewhere. As you can see, this is the same root problem but framed in a way which highlights the true business impact. The printer is still the root of the problem, but its impact on the business is substantial.

The other factor to consider whenever you are working to solve a problem is F.U.D. Fear, uncertainty, and doubt. F.U.D. is what makes it easier to take no action rather than to act. In short, it is the risk of deciding versus living with the devil you know. For some people, not deciding eliminates the risk of making a bad decision. It is the safe call. However, if you can create a compelling case for how a significant business issue can successfully be addressed, you will find decision makers more eager to act. The potential benefits will outweigh their concerns about the potential risk and motivate them to act.

You may find that during the discovery process, the prospect you are working with only sees the immediate problem. They only see the tip of the iceberg. They understand the impact to them or their team but may be unaware of the greater implications to their company. It is your job to assist them in seeing this clearly. You can help them get what they want, a new printer, by helping them present a case to management that the new printer is necessary to serve their clients and improve revenue generation and profitability. You can help them become the hero for seeing the true implications of the problem and how it negatively impacts the business overall. And as Jeffrey Gitomer says, "If you make a sale, you can earn a commission. If you make a friend, you can earn a fortune!"

The Importance of Taking Notes

Whenever you are meeting with someone you should be prepared to take notes to ensure you capture the critical information being shared. I have found taking notes with a pad and pen is preferred to a laptop or tablet. The reason I prefer the traditional way is to avoid any potential distractions with other apps or emails popping up. I always ask permission to take notes. When you are with a prospect or client, at the start of the conversation simply ask, "Would it be ok if I took some notes?" They always say yes. While it is a simple request, it is a powerful question on several levels. First, it is polite and indicates you want their permission to proceed. It defers authority to them, subconsciously making them feel more important while increasing your likeability. Second, it indicates what they are sharing with you is important and that you are going to listen intently and write it down. Be sure to capture their language, the words or phrases they use and that are indicative of their company or industry. You will benefit from using similar language when you develop your recommendation. In response, they will do two things. First, they will generally be more thoughtful with the information they disclose. Simply stated, the information shared is generally of higher quality. Second, they will speak slower to allow you the time necessary to capture the information.

There are additional benefits to this approach. When they are done speaking, take a moment to review your notes.

Then you will ask, "Would you mind if I review my notes with you to ensure I captured the information you provided correctly?" They always agree. Again, this signifies your interest to gain understanding and provides you the opportunity to do two important things. Quite frankly, this is where the 'selling' starts to happen. First, you will verify the information to ensure you did correctly document all the key points they shared. Second, and more importantly, it will allow you to qualify their answers to prioritize the information they provided and to align it to the best strengths of your offering. If they shared three must-have requirements, you want to get the prospect to rank them (1, 2, 3) in order of your offering's greatest strengths. You want alignment between what they want and what you can best offer them.

For example, if they offer three specific requirements for their application, you will work to prioritize the order to best align with the strengths of the solution you will most likely recommend. Here is the reason for approaching it this way. While you realize you can satisfy all three requirements, you also know your main competitor typically struggles with the third item mentioned. This is an opportunity to move this criterion to the top of the list to give your solution a competitive advantage. Here is sample exchange:

You: "I see you identified three key requirements. Items 1, 2, and 3. I have other clients who have found Item 3 to be of major importance. Do you feel this is true for you as well?"

Prospect: "Yes, I would say that requirement is most important."

You: "Good. And would you say that Item 2 is next in importance?"

Prospect: "Yes, that is true."

You: "Excellent. Let me make a note of the order of importance for these key factors."

Now, you may also have another capability which distinguishes you from your competitors and the prospect did not put it on the list. Now is the time to attempt to add that criterion into the list of priorities already provided. Remember, it is better to ask follow-up questions, to steer the conversation, than to make assumptions or statements. Guide the conversation by asking thoughtful questions so the prospect is the one telling you what they value. The dialogue continues:

You: "I noticed you did not mention XYZ as a consideration. However, I have collaborated with other clients who have considered this an important factor in the evaluation process. Do you think it is something you might want to evaluate as well?"

Prospect: "Interesting. I had not considered XYZ as necessary, but now that you mention it, I think it makes sense to include it as a requirement as well."

You: "Very well. I will add it as Item 4 on your list of requirements."

If the prospect does not want to include it as a requirement, no loss. You made the attempt, and this is what is important. Also, notice I did not say I offered a capability which my competition does not offer. Instead, I referred to it as a capability another client found to be important in their evaluation and decision-making process. This adds credibility to the suggestion, making it more likely to be well received and accepted. This will be another factor to tip the scales in your favor when the various solutions are compared and evaluated by the prospect and other stakeholders.

Every opportunity to interface with a prospect or client truly is a selling opportunity. What I hope you see is that you can do quite a bit of selling by asking pertinent and timely questions more effectively than you can by making statements or proclamations. Questions are powerful and allow the person asking the questions to steer the conversation while allowing the person answering the question to feel important and feel as if they are in control.

Learning Points:

1. Sales professionals rarely have issues closing business, they have a challenge conducting a thorough discovery process. The discovery process is the most important

part of the sales process since it will enable you to learn about a prospect's challenges, their fears, their desires, and how you can best help them. If you ask thoughtful questions, and listen carefully, they will tell you what you need to do to help them buy rather than trying to sell them.

2. Ask questions to uncover and develop explicit needs. Be sure to document each need and ensure you understand how each need is important to the various stakeholders who will influence the decision.

3. Prospects may not always understand the impact of a problem on their business. They may see the problem as a 'tree' and be unable to recognize the 'forest'. It is your job to help them make the connection and then assist them with developing a solid business case to get the challenge resolved. You can make them the hero of their own success story. Do not assume they know how to do this on their own. It is your job to show them.

4. Get beyond the obvious problem and find how the issue is really impacting them and their business. Find

the business implication to the issue. This is the issue that executives want to know about because they are responsible for minimizing negative impacts while maximizing their two main objectives: revenue growth and profitability. These are the problems they are motivated to address and if the return on investment can be clearly identified, it clears the way to a decision.

"Every sale has five basic obstacles: no need, no money, no hurry, no desire, no trust."

Zig Ziglar

"Care enough to create value for customers. If you get that part right, selling is easy."

Anthony Iannarino

Chapter 11: Presentations and Demonstrations

In many selling situations you may have the opportunity to make a presentation to a client or prospect about your offering. This can be an exciting time to display what you know. Do not fall into this trap. Remember, the old selling phrase, "show and sell, not show and tell" (Unknown). It is important to remember that everyone has a favorite radio station, and it is called WIIFM. WIIFM stands for "What's in it for me?" This is what your prospect or client is on the lookout for every time there is an interaction. You should be aware of this and plan your presentations and demonstrations accordingly. Staying focused on what is important to them will give you an advantage over your competitors who often see this as an invitation to talk about themselves. To speak about how wonderful their products or services are, how great their company is, what they do which is better than the rest. While this may appear important on the surface it is not important to the client. That is, unless you take the time and effort to craft your presentation in such a way as to make it meaningful to them. In most cases, sharing stories of successful past performance and the business outcomes you created for other clients, will help you demonstrate your ability to achieve a successful outcome for them.[26]

Presentations

It would be imprudent for me to tell you exactly how to construct a presentation for every conceivable situation you may encounter. Rather, I will attempt to provide you with some important concepts you will be able to utilize as appropriate. You may be fortunate to have a marketing department who has prepared various presentations for your use. This is a great start, but a word of caution. People in marketing are not in sales. They have a different mindset which may or may not include a high-performance sales

---

[26] Goodman, J.A. (2014, Aug. 12). *Customer Experience 3.0: High-Profit Strategies in the Age of Techno Service*. AMACOM.

professional mindset. If you plan to use some or all of what has already been created, please be sure to review it to ensure it includes these elements. Otherwise, it would be wise to make the necessary adjustments to ensure the presentation will cultivate an "I want to buy" reaction.

The Power of Questions

We have already spoken about the power of great questions. Questions are what allows us to gather information and to better understand what our prospect is thinking and feeling, so we can best present our offering to create maximum value. While a presentation may suggest this is a time for you to do all the talking, it is really another opportunity to get your prospect talking by incorporating great questions. This approach will allow you to validate what you already know, tie that understanding to your capabilities, and gain confirmation you are creating value for the prospect. You will want to do this early and often as part of a process that continually reinforces the benefits and value of your solution.

Let us suppose you have been involved with a prospect for some time and they have invited you to present your recommendation to a small group of decision influencers who will be involved in making the final selection. You have met with only one or two of these individuals previously, but the group you will present to is composed of five people. During your initial meetings you have inquired about the needs and goals of the other stakeholders. However, you have not heard from them directly. Early in the presentation is a great time to validate what you know and to discover if there is anything else which might be important.

Here is a sample slide which you may find helpful:

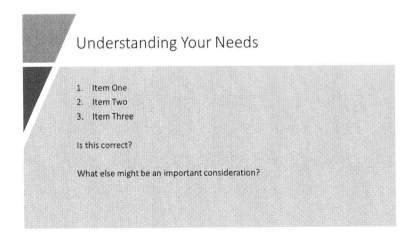

Here you list the significant elements you have been told are important during your previous meetings conducting the discovery process. Then, you ask for confirmation. You want to make sure what you think is critical is, in fact, critical. Next, take the opportunity to inquire if there is anything else to include or if anything has changed since you last spoke. It is a simple gesture, but a powerful one.

This is the time, before you launch into the presentation, to ensure you highlight what is truly important to every member of the group and any additional stakeholders who may not be present. Hopefully, you will find the group offers some other considerations. Take the time to write them down on a notepad you have handy. If they offer two new items, be sure to take the time to pose follow up questions about how these items are important, just as you would do during the discovery phase. In truth, you are always in the discovery phase when it comes to gathering important information. Then, once you have all the items listed, you will want to prioritize the items in order of importance. This is a selling opportunity for you. If there are now five items listed, and you do one of these items especially well, you will want to try to get the prospect to indicate this one as the most important criterion. Here is an example:

You: "Thank you all for helping me create a list of the most important considerations. I see you have identified Item 4, which appears to be a key factor. Would you agree this is the most important of the five items listed?"

Prospects: "Yes, Item 4 is critically important to us."

You: "Great. Now, I also see you have included Item 1 from our earlier discussions. Would you consider this the next important requirement?"

Prospects: "Yes. Followed by Item 5 and then Item 2."

You: "Wonderful. So, we have, in order of importance, Items 4, 1, 5, 2, and 3. Is that correct?"

Prospects: "Yes, that is correct."

Here is the importance of this exercise. First, you have verified what is important. Second, you have gotten the prospect to prioritize the items to align to your greatest strengths. And third, and perhaps most important, you have gotten the prospects engaged in a dialogue. You have them participating in the presentation rather than being passive or just listening to what you have to say. Engaging their participation early will encourage their continued participation throughout the presentation. It will provide you important feedback, and the opportunity to fine-tune your presentation, for maximum impact as you proceed.

You may be wondering what to do if you do not have every item as part of your preconstructed presentation. Do not worry about that right now. It is far more important to understand what they think is important. Start with what they have told you is the most important item to review. Again, look to engage the prospects in the discussion as much as you provide information. For example:

You: "You indicated Item 4, ease of operation, is a key component for you. I would like to take a moment to share with you how we accomplish this in our solution. We integrate an easy-to-use interface, with professional training upon installation, coupled with ongoing support to answer questions or offer you help when you need it."

(This is providing them some information about your system and your approach for helping them get up to speed with its use. Now you want to ask a question to engage them.)

You: "Does this approach meet your expectations?" or "Does this approach align with your expectations for an easy-to-use system?"

This is the pattern you will want to utilize during the presentation. You will provide information related to what is most important to them, and then you will validate what you have provided to ensure it hits the mark dead center. If the prospect fails to acknowledge they are satisfied, or does so only half-heartedly, stop right there. You want an enthusiastic confirmation, not a simple 'I guess so'. This response is the equivalent to a 'no'. Ask the prospect to share with you their concerns about what you presented. For example, "I'm sensing you are not entirely satisfied with the item presented. Could you tell me what concerns you, please?" When the prospect answers, you are back in discovery mode. Write down their concern, qualify it with follow-up questions as appropriate, and address their concern to the best of your ability. If it is something you cannot answer, let them know you will have to do some additional research, to ensure the issue is properly addressed. Be sure to ask them if this is acceptable. Then confirm they are satisfied before you proceed. It is far wiser to acknowledge when you don't know the answer than to make something up. If you are honest with them, chances are good that they will respect you being forthcoming. Plus, your overall believability will increase because you have proven to the prospect you are not afraid to say, "I'm not sure, but I will find out." Believability improves trust and trust is the foundation for all mutually-beneficial relationships.

Let us review the implications of the preceding conversation.

1. The prospect identifies something important you can do and, perhaps, do better than anyone else. Wonderful! You learn it is important and how it is important to them. Now, you have another reason to justify choosing your solution for their organization when they evaluate their options.

2. The prospect identifies something important that you cannot do. It may be something none of your competitors can provide either. Then the item is of no real consequence. There are times when a prospect may offer an idea which is not available, and it is nothing more than a "pie in the sky" wish. You can simply acknowledge it, write it down, and move on.

3. However, you may have just learned from the individual who proposed the need that it is a capability your competitor offers, and they knew about it. They may even have known that you do not offer the same capability as a way of identifying a potential reason to saying 'no' to your offering. They could have even been coached by your competitor to bring this deficiency to light to create a reason for not select your offering. This

is where probing, "How is this important to you?" is critical. Expose the rationale behind the need so you can appropriately address it. You may learn it is only important to this person and not the group in general. In which case you can diminish its significance on the decision overall.

In any case, you are gaining additional information as you are making your presentation. You will not always be able to do everything they want; however, your goal is to continuously highlight the things you can do and work to have the prospect prioritize these capabilities as the must-have items for their solution. In very few cases will your offering have exactly every capability a prospect requires or desires. It is fine since most other providers will be facing a similar challenge. Your goal is to focus on what you do best and to get them to want those things above anything else.

As you proceed with the presentation, you will want to ensure you continually align your offering to meet or exceed their stated needs and goals. For example, if they identified the need to produce 100 widgets per hour, and your device can produce 110 widgets per hour, be sure to highlight the fact. Then ask, "Is this additional productivity of value to you?" If so, "How might the added productivity be helpful to you and your business?" The fact that your device produces 10% faster output is great, but only if you can tie it to something which makes it significant to the prospect. If you are unable to establish this connection, what you see as an advantage is not an advantage at all. Do not assume that every unique capability you offer is an advantage to your prospect. You must understand how it could provide an advantage and present it to them in the form of question. For example, "While you did not indicate the need to produce 110 widgets per hour, would this additional production capacity be a benefit to you?" Ask and confirm. If the prospect acknowledges it would be a benefit, ask them how. Write it down and qualify the answer fully to capture all the value this will create for the prospect. If this capability is now recognized as a legitimate benefit, you will want to cultivate this into a competitive advantage to help distinguish your offering from other potential solutions.

This process will also help you understand what your competition may be doing when they have the opportunity to present their offering. As noted in the example above, if the base requirement is to produce 100 widgets per hour, and your device meets but does not exceed this explicit requirement, and you know that your competitor's solution is faster, capable of producing 115 widgets per hour, you need to explore how this might influence their decision? You may know the competitor has an advantage when it comes to production speed, but you also know the added productivity comes with an additional expense. Perhaps to achieve the additional output their solution is going to be 15% more expensive than the solution you are offering. If the prospect does not see an advantage to the higher output speed, and all other factors are equal, you may have an advantage in terms of overall return on investment since your solution is less expensive. Again, you want to stay away from broad assumptions.

This is part of the reason learning about your competition and industry is of vital importance. Take the time to ask good questions and to qualify the responses so you know in absolute terms the situation. This same scenario could have dramatically different results given two completely different prospects. If all the other factors are equal, the production speed may sway one prospect to prefer it and the another to dismiss it. You want to operate in the world of facts, both rational and emotional, and not assumptions or preconceived notions. Ask questions to validate your understanding of the facts in the mind of the prospect.

When your presentation is complete, take the time to confirm once again what you know. Go back to the key needs and confirm that each has been thoroughly addressed and there are no additional questions or concerns about your ability to satisfy the stated criteria. For example:

You: "I would like to ensure we have addressed all of your requirements. As noted earlier, you said these five items were most important to you. Is this correct?"

Prospect: "Yes, that is correct."

You: "Great. Have I addressed each of these items to your satisfaction? Do you have any remaining questions or concerns about what we discussed today?"

Prospect: "No, everything made sense."

You: "Perfect. Now, has anything changed as a result of this presentation and our discussion? Are there any new items we may need to discuss?"

Prospect: "No."

If the prospect says 'yes' you will need to go back to discovery mode to learn how this is important and see if you can address it now or if you will require additional time to make a recommendation. You want to continually uncover any information that will influence the buying and decision-making process. Why guess when you can simply ask?

It may be difficult to know if you are the only person making a presentation to a group or if they have scheduled multiple companies to present their offerings. You will find that prospects share this information to varying degrees. However, if you have developed an internal 'coach' during the sales process, you may be able to gain an inside perspective and further influence the process. If you are given the choice, request to go either first or last if there are multiple presentations being scheduled. You do not want to get lost in the middle. If you go first, you can set the bar by which the remaining presenters will be judged. If you go last, you will have the opportunity to leave a lasting impression in the prospect's mind.

A 'coach' is an asset to have in every sales situation. It is a person either inside or outside the prospect's organization who can provide you useful insights on the culture, process, people, personalities, and other factors that may influence the buying or decision-making process. It should, as a natural result, influence your approach from a sales process perspective. An external coach can be anyone with cardinal knowledge of your prospect and their business. For example, another sales professional from your leads group may have experience collaborating with them. This may be a resource for a strategic introduction or a positive reference. Further, they can share with you their experiences and how what approach they found most effective.

While external coaches are useful, having an internal coach is even more powerful. Often this coach will be the person who can champion your solution and build consensus around approving your recommendation because they have a vested interest. If you are fortunate to establish a great relationship with someone inside the company, you may find this person an ongoing resource with access to behind-the-scenes information essential to your mutual success. What other competitors are involved? Who are the key decision influencers? How is your offering being received by the various stakeholders? All these items are critical to navigating the sales process, the buying process, and the decision-making process.

Demonstrations

A demonstration is simply another form of a presentation. You will want to approach it in a similar fashion.

Demonstrations often occur when you are selling a physical product, like a machine or device, and the prospect wants to see it in operation. However, you may also perform a demonstration in the form of a site visit where a prospect comes to your facility, or to visit a client site, to see firsthand how you perform a certain service. Either way, it is important to remember this is key selling opportunity. The objective is to create a demonstration which clearly shows, and proves, exactly how your offering will best satisfy their explicit needs and goals. It is a proof of performance opportunity.

When conducting a demonstration, you may have the opportunity to bring your prospect to your office or an existing client site. Your office is a controlled environment. It will allow you to ensure everything is working and set up for a most conducive experience. However, taking a prospect to a client site can offer additional benefits. First, the prospect will be able to see your product or service operating in a real-world environment. Second, if the client is an advocate for you, your company, and your product, there is the opportunity for your prospect to hear directly from a raving fan. It is a powerful opportunity to interject a strong recommendation and further validate the benefits you can create. I have found some clients are so good at presenting the value we created for them, they do most of the selling for me. And to be honest, the prospect is much more receptive to hearing what they are being told by the client as compared to anything I might say. It is important to recognize this reality and allow your clients to help you close more deals.

If you decide to visit a client site to perform a demonstration, there are a few things you will want to do to ensure a great experience:

1. Client permission and availability. In addition to confirming your client is amenable to your coming to their facility, make sure they will be personally available to attend at least the beginning of the demonstration. This will be an opportunity to make introductions and for your client to make any comments about you, your company, and the product

or service. This may also encourage them to stay for the duration and function as an advocate for your offering.

2. Verify the performance of the device being demonstrated. If it is something that requires maintenance, request that your service department go there the day prior to give it a review. Let them know you will be using the device for a presentation. You will want to ensure that everything is working perfectly. If it is a service and you have personnel on site, be sure to let them know you will be bringing a prospective client for a visit. Make sure everyone is dressed their best and all workspaces are tidy. Let them know they are an important part of the presentation.

3. Availability of supplies. Make sure your client has whatever consumables might be necessary to present the device. Offer to have items shipped prior to avoid wasting their inventory. You client will appreciate your consideration. For a service, consider what the staff might be doing at the time of day you plan to visit.

Coordinate with your team lead on site to ensure their work can be visible to the prospect.

4. If the device is used as part of a larger manufacturing process, you may not be able to provide supplies, and will have to have your prospect understand the device is in use during the visit. You may not be able to show certain features or functionality if it is in use for a specific purpose. Ensure this is acceptable. Often there is more to gain seeing the product in use than what can be seen in a showroom environment. For a service, make sure your staff is aware they might be asked a question by the prospect. Some prospects want to hear from the people performing the service. Make sure your team is prepared and comfortable interfacing with the prospect.

5. After the demonstration, be sure to send a handwritten note and small gift of appreciation to your client for allowing you to visit their facility. This is another opportunity to build a strong relationship and

demonstrate your gratitude for their efforts on your behalf. If you make a sale because of their assistance, go a step further an invite them to lunch to celebrate. Your gesture will be appreciated. In the case of a service demonstration, don't forget to thank your team on site for their participation.

I recommend you start the demonstration in the same fashion as discussed in the presentation. Identify the known needs and see if there are any new or additional needs or objectives which may be important to the prospect or other stakeholders. Has anything changed since your last discussion? You should take advantage of every opportunity to gather and validate information that may prove useful for positioning your offering as the best value and solution for your prospect.

One of the biggest dangers to a demonstration is the desire, as with a presentation, to show too much. Let's face it, you are excited to have a well-qualified prospect in the office, ready to see how your product can best satisfy their needs.

You want to show them everything it can do, especially the capabilities or features no one else offers. This is another trap called 'over-selling'. Stay focused on what your prospect has identified as their key buying criteria. Prioritize those items and present in order of importance. If, along the journey, your client says, "This is perfect. I want it!" stop there. If they are ready to buy, let them buy. Do not "buy it back" by continuing along because you have not had the opportunity to show them every feature or capability. You have no idea what may happen next. Be thankful you received a buy confirmation and end the demonstration with, "That is fantastic. Let me get the contract for you to sign." I have seen more damage done by over-selling than from under-selling a solution. Remember, it is about their experience, not yours. While you may be disappointed to not have shown them all the cool features offered, I hope cashing that big commission check more than compensates you for this minor inconvenience.

The Details Matter

Whether you are creating a written recommendation, presentation, or demonstration, be sure you have your work reviewed by someone else who has an eye for good content, proper spelling, and grammar. There is nothing worse than a prospect or client reading your document or looking at a slide only to discover errors. You are a professional. They rightfully expect professionalism. Little things like spelling and grammatical errors create a distraction. Instead of staying focused to what you want to share and discuss, they are now looking for the next error you may have committed. Always ask a trusted co-worker or member of your support team to review your work to ensure you are promoting a professional image. What you create speaks about you and your company. Be sure you are consistently promoting the right message.

Learning Points:

1. A presentation is another opportunity to ask great questions. Validate your understanding early and work to solicit any additional needs before launching your presentation.

2. Be sure to understand how any new criteria is important. Prioritize all known needs to best position

your offering as the strongest solution to their stated needs and goals.

3. Identify a coach to assist you. An internal coach is preferred since they can become a champion for your solution, providing you critical information while actively promoting your solution as the preferred choice.

4. Use the checklist to arrange a demonstration at an existing client site. While it can be a little more challenging, it offers you the opportunity to receive a testimonial from a happy client – a powerful message to help you sell.

"The 5 P's: Proper Planning Prevents Poor Performance."
James Baker

"Everyone has an invisible sign hanging from their neck saying, 'Make me feel important.' Never forget this message when working with people."

Mary Kay Ash

Chapter 12: Creating Winning Recommendations

Far too often I see salespeople present their offering in an estimate, quote, or proposal. Makes sense. In my opinion, these salespeople are not sales professionals. Professionals make recommendations. They bring their years of experience and expertise to someone with a unique or a specific problem, providing a call to action designed to help them. Yes, that is what professionals do. And that is what you will want to do as well. Here is another interesting psychological fact. We are conditioned to accept recommendations from experts. Growing up, we have been told to accept professional recommendations from doctors, accountants, and attorneys. Why should this not apply to our profession as well?

Let me ask you a question. What is the purpose of a recommendation? Why do we create and present them to a prospect? What does it do? If you answered to provide the details of the offering, such as the price, the terms and conditions, and other technical specifications, you are correct. This is certainly a component of a good recommendation. However, is this the essential purpose of the document? No. The purpose of a written recommendation is to 'sell' for you when you are not there. That is the real purpose of a recommendation. It is a document that outlines your offering and clearly demonstrates the value you create for the stakeholders and their company. It effectively communicates this message even when you are not present to do so yourself. A great recommendation conveys a compelling story. Stories are not only more enjoyable to absorb but are actually easier for the human brain to remember.[27]

Now, I understand the effort required to develop a winning recommendation is significant, which is the original reason

---

[27] Pink, D.H. (2006, Mar. 7). A Whole New Mind: Why Right-Brainers Will Rule the Future. Riverhead Books.

templates were created. What I would recommend is that you determine as early in the sales process as possible if a particular opportunity is worth your very best efforts or not. Is a particular opportunity and relationship worth the time and effort required to be successful? If it is, then great. You will see the time and effort as an investment in building a mutually-beneficial relationship and developing a new client. If it is not, then do yourself a favor and pass. Provide the opportunity to another salesperson on your team or just walk away. Do not invest your time where you will not do your best work to win the business. You do a disservice to your prospect as well as to yourself.

While most organizations have templates to assist in structuring a recommendation, you must be certain you personalize the document for each specific prospect. There is nothing worse than a prospect realizing they are reading a template. It diminishes any feeling of being unique and special, and people will resent it.[28] Further, it shows them, despite your earlier statements of being caring and

---

[28] Blount, J. (2011, Nov. 15). *People Follow You: The Real Secret to What Matters Most in Leadership*. Wiley.

engaged, that you really think they are just another opportunity to make a sale. All your hard work in the interactions leading up to this point can be compromised if you fail to take the final steps to demonstrate how you can solve their unique challenge and make their life better. Remember, when you can generate a positive emotional response from a prospect, you increase the likelihood you will secure an affirmative decision and sale.[29]

There are several simple, but highly effective ways you can personalize a template to ensure the document speaks to the prospect's specific situation and makes them feel as if the recommendation was prepared exclusively for them. You want to customize the recommendation to demonstrate your interest in helping them resolve their unique challenges and realize the benefits you have discussed. Now is the time to put the story into written format to clearly articulate all the details of the problem, how it will be solved, and the benefits which will be realized by acting now.

---

[29] Postema, D.H. (2013, Aug. 20). *Psychology of Sales: From Average to Rainmaker.* CreateSpace Independent Publishing Platform.

Among the components of an effective recommendation are the following:

- Current State, Proposed State, Future State Analysis
  - Define the challenge (problem) or the opportunity for improvement (gain) and be sure to use the language used by the stakeholders.
  - What action are you proposing?
  - How will this action create value by achieving the stated goals and objectives?
- Benefits to Be Realized and Achieved (The Value You Will Create)
  - List in order of importance, be as specific as possible, and be sure to accentuate the uniqueness of your offering in creating this value.
  - May include saving time or money, reducing effort or minimizing downtime, ease of use and less frustrations, or improvements in generating new revenue streams or increasing profitability.
- Return on Investment (ROI) Calculations
  - Demonstrate how the investment will pay for itself over time.

- o   Include both hard dollars and soft dollars.
- o   Hard Dollars – the amount you will save each month or each time you utilize the service, or how new revenue and profits will offset the investment in your solution.
- o   Soft Dollars – the potential savings in time, effort, or quality.
- Proof of Performance – Why Buy You?
  - o   How have you implemented this solution before and what results have been achieved?
- Financial Investment
  - o   Outline the investment required in terms of either a purchase price, a lease, or payment schedule for specific services.
  - o   Do not undersell your offering. A superior brand can charge a 10% to 20% premium.[30]
- References
  - o   Who can testify to your ability to achieve the results promised? Who have you or your company previously helped who would share their positive experiences?

---

[30] Kotler, P. (2005, May 5). *According to Kotler: The World's Foremost Authority on Marketing Answers Your Questions.* AMACOM.

- Terms and Conditions
  - o Any important details about the recommendation, acquisition process, support, service, or other important considerations.

Depending on what you sell, you may want to consider including photos of the prospect's office, facility, or production area as appropriate. Always be sure to gain permission from the prospect before you take any photos. If the prospect is agreeable, there are few things more powerful for stakeholders to see that level of personalization in your recommendation. You can also include appropriate images of your product or service to relate the benefits to the prospect's unique situation. It should not be a marketing 'puff' piece, but a very targeted document to how you will create value for the prospect and help them achieve their goals. Remember, prospects often have a difficult time assessing value.[31] You need to clearly articulate the value you are creating for them and state it in your recommendation. Never assume that the benefits

---

[31] Porter, M.E. (1998, Jun. 1). *Competitive Advantage: Creating and Sustaining Superior Performance*. Free Press.

are obvious. State them accurately in your recommendation so the value you create is clear and compels action.

An effective recommendation also becomes an important tool for your coach or champion to utilize when presenting your offer to the other stakeholders and working to gain final approval for your solution. Even though you have discussed and enumerated the reasons why a prospect should accept your recommendation, do not assume it is clear and easily memorable to everyone involved in the decision-making process. Use the recommendation to highlight each benefit as well as the return on investment so there is no question as to the value you are creating for the prospect. Assumption is the mother of all screw ups. Do not assume anything when you can carefully articulate it in your recommendation and follow-up conversations with your prospect. Remember, people buy drills because they want holes, not because they want another power tool.

Price versus Cost

There will certainly be times when you present your recommendation complete with a compelling reason for action and a substantial return on investment only to hear from the prospect that "the price is too high." In some cases, this is a result of their perception of the value. Or it may be the result of comparing your recommendation to a competitive offering. It can be extremely frustrating in situations where you know that your solution is better than what your competitor is offering. However, your prospect wants the value you are creating for the lower price being offered.

In this situation, you may want to consider asking the prospect what is more important to them: the price or the cost. At first glance, you may be wondering what's the difference? Well, there is a difference, and it is essential for you to be confident in the difference in order to impact your prospect's thinking. This is about changing your prospect's mindset and dislodging the idea that your recommendation can be obtained for a lower price point.

Let's review an example. While there is no guarantee that the conversation will go exactly as presented, I can tell you that myself and my sales team have used this approach numerous times with great success. This is further proof of the importance of the discovery process and creating a winning recommendation. It is only by knowing the real motivation for the prospect to act, and capturing that information in your recommendation, that you can remind them what they told you. It isn't that you are convincing them of something, rather, it is a process of reminding them what they originally told you. And, unless something dramatic has changed, why would they abandon their own thinking on the subject?

Prospect: "I like what you have to offer, but your competitor is offering a very similar solution at substantially less money. Quite frankly, your price is just too high."

You: "When you say the price, you are referring to the initial investment, correct?"

Prospect: "Yes. The purchase price is too high."

You: "Okay, let me ask you a question. Which is of greater concern to you, the price or the cost?"

Prospect: (Pause) "What do you mean? What's the difference?"

You: "I'm curious to know which is more important to you. The price, which is the upfront investment of the recommended solution, or the cost, which is the long-term expense of the solution?"

Prospect: (Another pause) "I'm not exactly certain. What's the difference?"

You: "The price is the upfront investment. The cost is the expense over time, including the potential risk that the solution will not deliver the results you want to achieve."

Prospect: "Interesting. Tell me more."

You: "Well, when we were discussing potential solutions to your challenge, you identified three key factors you said would be the basis of your decision. Is that accurate?"

Prospect: "Yes, that is true."

You: "Has anything about those critical factors changed?"

Prospect: "No."

You: "Let me ask you this question, how did the competition address each of those points in their proposal?"

Prospect: "Well, they really didn't. They provided me a quote for a similar product (or service) to the one you proposed. I'm assuming that these items are pretty much the same or at least comparable."

You: "Well, that's interesting. What you're basically telling me is that they provided you a 'me too!' proposal. You and I spent considerable time to review your current challenges, discussed how best to implement a new approach, identified what success would look like, and developed a recommendation based on your unique situation. What you're telling me now is that the competition didn't do that. They just offered you a price that was lower than our investment amount and you are assuming they can achieve the same results. Is that correct?"

Prospect: "Well, yes. That's true."

You: "Let me ask you another question. Do you really want to accept the risk associated with a company that is basing their entire offering on a claim of 'me too'?"

Prospect: "No, I don't want the risk. I need to ensure that this project is a success."

You: "Yes, that's what you told me in the beginning. You said there was a great deal of internal focus on this project, and you needed to ensure that the solution implemented achieved the stated goals. Have I demonstrated that our offering would achieve those goals along with a substantial return on investment with minimal risk?"

Prospect: "Yes, you have."

You: "Then why would you want to risk the success of this project working with anyone but me?"

Prospect: "Well, I had not considered it from that perspective. Perhaps you're right. Your competitor hasn't demonstrated the same insights or proven that they can achieve the same results. Under further consideration, I am going to do business with you."

I hope you see that the talk track is based on having a very clear understanding of the prospect's requirements, priorities, and goals. Information you should have uncovered during the discovery process and used when presenting your recommendation to prove that your offering would best meet the criteria. Now, you are essentially reminding the prospect of what they told you was important and asking if your competitor went through the same process, or if they simply based their proposal on some assumptions without providing ample proof of their ability to achieve the same outcome.

In nearly every case where either I or a team member had a discussion with a prospect, we discovered that the competitor did not display the same due diligence we did during the engagement. They simply gathered some basic information, including the fact that we were providing a recommendation, and went back to their office and 'slapped' together a half-baked quote with a lower price point. Their entire strategy was to say 'me too' at a lower price. While this can sometimes work in their favor, it is up to you to thwart that behavior by confronting the prospect with the facts and asking them point blank if they want to really work with such a lazy salesperson. Or would they prefer to work with a professional businessperson who fully understands their challenges, who has provided insightful expert advice, and then presented a comprehensive recommendation that will help them achieve their goals, as you have done. You will find that after further consideration, if you have done all these things well, you are the best choice.

 Visit www.practical-sales-wisdom.com to access the **Winning Recommendations Game Planner**.

Learning Points:

1. When you create a recommendation for a prospective client, remember that they are expecting a document that speaks to their unique situation. Everyone wants to be treated as special. Presenting someone with a template that speaks in general terms is insulting.

2. Your recommendation must be compelling on an emotional level as much as it is logical. Remember,

people make decisions based on emotions and emotions drive action. While you want the recommendation to be factual and logical it must be compelling on an emotional level.

3. When a prospect comments about your price being too high, challenge them with the "Is it the price or the cost?" question. Don't be afraid to challenge their thinking and use the information they provided you during the discovery process to remind them of what they said was most important to them.

"The success of your presentation will be judged not by the knowledge you send but by what the listener receives."

Lilly Walters

"Our greatest weakness lies in giving up. The most certain way to succeed is always to try just one more time."

Thomas A. Edison

Chapter 13: Follow Up, Follow Up, Follow Up

I find it amazing how much has been written about the importance of follow up. You would think one or two books would be sufficient. No. There is literally an endless array of material dedicated to the art of follow up and nearly every sales book discusses it at length. Then why, you might ask, does the average salesperson struggle so intensely with this concept? The answer is simple. We have become a society of instant gratification. We no longer value hard work but expect instant success. If it takes more than a moment or two, most people are not interested. Here are some interesting statistics on follow up:[32]

- 80% of sales require five follow-up calls after the first meeting
- 44% of sales reps give up after one follow-up
- After four follow-ups, 94% of salespeople have given up

Let's take a moment to digest these important facts. The first one is just amazing. Nearly half (44%) of salespeople give up after one follow up. How crazy is this? Here we are, as sales professionals, actively looking for prospects for our products or services. We finally come across one and have an initial interaction (discussion). Then, 44% of the time we follow up once and then just walk away and give up. Now consider that 80% of sales require five follow ups but 94% of sales professionals give up after four. This means that

[32]Loew, I. (n.d.). *The Art of the Sales Follow-Up: 7 Ways to Keep the Conversation Going*. HubSpot. Retrieved Jan. 31, 2022, from https://blog.hubspot.com/sales/sales-follow-up-infographic; Williams, B. (n.d.). *21 Mind-Blowing Sales Stats*. Brevet. Retrieved Jan. 31, 2022, from https://blog.thebrevetgroup.com/21-mind-blowing-sales-stats

only six percent of sales professionals are willing to do what it takes to make the vast majority of sales. If you're not willing to do what it takes then you are simply wasting your time. While this information is interesting, it is also powerful in the sense of what your competition is, or is not, doing in most cases. And remember, your competitors are not just the salespeople in your industry, but salespeople across all industries who are calling on the same point of contacts (those influencers and decision makers) you want to engage.

Follow Up Rule #1. Never end an interaction with a prospect or client without first determining and scheduling the next interaction. It does not matter whether you are on a phone call, a video call, or meeting in person. Before that meeting ends, it is YOUR responsibility to secure the next appointment and denote the next step in the process to keep the opportunity moving forward. If you fail to do this small act, you may find yourself spending countless hours calling, emailing, and sending carrier pigeons to schedule the next interaction you could easily have scheduled when you were with the person at that time. This is one of the keys to your success, and it is easy to do. Here is an example:

You: "Well Mr. Prospect, thank you for your time today. Just to recap, you have agreed to speak with your supervisor to ensure there are ample funds available to proceed, and I am to finalize the recommendation with a few changes for your approval. Is that correct?"

Prospect: "Yes, that sounds correct to me."

You: "Excellent. While we are together, can we please take a moment to check our calendars to schedule a convenient time to follow up? Are you available next Tuesday or would Wednesday be more convenient?"

Prospect: "I am available next Tuesday in the morning."

You: "Great. Does 9:00 AM or 11:00 AM work better for you on Tuesday?"

Prospect: "11:00 AM sounds good."

You: "Good. Then I will come to your office next Tuesday at 11:00 AM. I will send you a calendar invitation right now to confirm. Thank you."

It is simple process, and it eliminates the potential hassle of scheduling the next meeting after you leave. You will save yourself an immeasurable amount of time and frustration securing next step appointments before you conclude the current interaction. Remember, confirm the next step as well as the next interaction before your current meeting ends to keep the sales process moving forward. This also lets you qualify the prospect further before your meeting ends. If the prospect is hesitant, or unwilling to schedule the next meeting, it should indicate there is an issue. Now is the best time to identify the challenge so you can address it before you conclude. For example:

You: "Well Mr. Prospect, thank you for your time today. You have agreed to speak with your supervisor to ensure there are funds available to proceed, and I am to finalize the recommendation for your consideration. Is this correct?"

Prospect: "Well, I'm not sure that will work."

You: "Really? Is there something I missed or is there something concerning you?"

Prospect: "Well, yes. I'm not sure my supervisor is going to be interested in spending the funds necessary to implement your solution."

You: "Interesting. What makes you think this is the case?"

Prospect: "I'm just not sure the justification is sufficient to generate his support."

You: "OK. I understand. We would not want to engage your supervisor if we cannot provide him the level of justification necessary to move forward. Perhaps we could take a few minutes to review the return on investment we discussed earlier to see if we have identified all the key points. Would this be helpful?"

Prospect: "Yes, that might be a good idea."

You: "Perfect. Let's start at the beginning so you will be properly prepared to discuss the recommendation with your supervisor. I will make some notes, so we will have a complete list of all the key points. Would this be acceptable to you?"

Prospect: "Yes, this sounds like a good idea."

You: "Great. Let's get to work."

Now you have identified a potential issue and you can properly address the challenge before the meeting concludes. Here is a sales truth for you. Often salespeople are most happy not knowing about a challenge which will prevent the sales cycle from moving forward. I know it sounds counterintuitive. But remember, over 90% of the sales professionals out there are going through the motions with no little or no interest in becoming a top performer. To them, ending the meeting with the hope of setting up a follow-up meeting is a success. However, when you are a top performer, you would never accept this as success. No, you want to know what is going on. You want to know about every possible issue or challenge so you can act. As Jimmy McGinty says in *The Replacements*, "Winners always want the ball...when the game is on the line."

This approach will provide you another opportunity to schedule the follow-up meeting to ensure you keep the sales process moving forward. Momentum plays a critical role in the sales process. It takes effort and energy to get the process moving. So, once it is moving, you want to build momentum and keep it moving. Otherwise, you will have start and stops which cause significant delays and force you to expend a great deal of energy to get the process moving again. So, if the prospect agrees to a new date for the follow-up meeting, you have satisfied their concerns. If they hesitate again, go back, and make inquiries to understand what challenge or concerns remain unresolved. Keep digging until to find the real reason they are hesitant to schedule the follow-up meeting. Do not accept maybe. We want to be in the 'yes' or 'no' business. The 'maybe' business is a world of muck for the 90% crowd.

Now, back to the statistics presented earlier. You can see how few sales are made in the first few interactions. Only 20% of all sales are made in four or less interactions. If you sell a simple product or service, you may only need one or two appointments to secure a decision. However, most B2B engagements are more complex and require substantially more interactions to secure a decision. Most are made with five to 12 follow-up interactions. While this is not a rule, per se, I think you will agree it is essential to plan each follow up activity to ensure you keep your opportunity moving forward.

Learning Points:

1. Most sales cycles take longer to close than one or two calls. You need to ensure you are diligent in following up with your prospects. It's always a good idea to gain commitment before the call or meeting ends when it would make sense to follow up. Schedule that next activity on your calendar and send the prospect a meeting invitation to ensure you keep on track.

2. The fact that most sales professionals do not follow up with prospects is an advantage for anyone who will follow up consistently. Don't rely on your memory if a prospect tells you, it isn't a good time, but call back in 60 days. Put it in your CRM system or on calendar. When you call them back remind them, they told you to follow up and you did so precisely. They should appreciate your diligence and follow through. You will establish credibility.

3. You always want to know the truth. Don't let a prospect demonstrate 'kindness' by not telling you the truth. Make it a point to qualify a lack of commitment and get to the truth. It's better to know they are not

interested so you can invest your time with someone who will value you and the value you can create.

"Our chief want in life is somebody who shall make us do what we can."

Ralph Waldo Emerson

Section 3: The Art of Selling

"Ability is what you're capable of doing. Motivation determines what you do. Attitude determines how well you do it."

Lou Holtz

Chapter 14: The Psychology of Selling

There has been a significant amount of wonderful information written about the psychology of selling. I think the acknowledgement of psychology in the world of professional selling has altered the way the top-performing sales professionals approach their business and their craft. While the concepts have been around for many years, I have seen an emergence of this focus in the last 10 years. It makes perfect sense. Despite all you hear about selling, especially B2B (business-to-business), it is essentially a P2P process (person-to-person). The adage that you never get a second chance to make a good first impression is true.

People make an instant judgement when they first meet someone.[33] You may be wondering why psychology is important to sales. Let us start our discussion here.

As presented earlier, there are different processes happening concurrently with every engagement. There is the sales process, the buying process, and the decision-making process. The decision-making process speaks specifically to how individuals and multiple individuals (or groups or committees) will come to a decision. It has a lot to do with how we think, feel, process information, and evaluate what is in our best interest. I like to tell my sales teams that everyone has a favorite radio station. It is called WIIFM – What's In It For Me. It is a reminder to them that this question is continually at the forefront of everyone's subconscious mind every moment of every day. It is innate and essential to our very being. As Daniel H. Pink commented, "In an age of abundance, appealing only to

---

[33] Blount, J. (2010, Jun. 21). *People Buy You: The Real Secret to What Matters Most in Business*. Wiley.

rational, logical, and functional needs is woefully insufficient."[34]

What makes psychology integral to sales is understanding how humans, your potential prospects, and clients think and feel about the world around them. You will enter this world, often as an uninvited guest, and you will want to properly navigate it in order to build a relationship, which leads to creating a client. Even in business-to-business sales, you are, in the end, working to have an individual, a person, decide to do business with you. There is all this talk about selling to companies. This is a misnomer. I have never witnessed a company buy anything. However, I have seen people buy products and services for a particular company. It is essential to understand how people think and feel so you can positively influence both the rational and emotional dimensions of their being to maximize your opportunity to develop a new client.

---

[34] Pink, D.H. (2005, Mar. 24). *A Whole New Mind: Why Right-Brainers Will Rule the Future*. Riverhead Books.

There may be people who say using psychology is a form of manipulation. I do not agree. As a sales professional you will be interacting with all types of people daily. It is critical for you to have a clear understanding of how they think and feel to work to develop a positive relationship with each person. You will have various people who either directly or indirectly influence a decision to grant you access to ask questions, to make a recommendation, and, eventually, to be considered as a partner for their business. In each interaction, you will either be building a case to work with you or not. Every interaction will create an impression. You want every impression to be positive and demonstrate your desire to provide a great solution for each stakeholder who will evaluate you, your company, and your solution. If using psychology can assist you with accomplishing this goal, then it would be foolish not to utilize this knowledge. Knowledge is power. The world is a very competitive place. You should take advantage of every opportunity to tilt the scales in your favor.

Since there are several well-known authors who have written comprehensive books about the psychology of sales, I will not attempt to replicate all the available information in this chapter. My favorite authors on this subject include John Asher and Jeb Blount. Each has made a significant contribution to the subject, and I think you will find their work comprehensive, informative, and actionable. I highly recommend you read their works on the subject to enhance your understanding and to develop skills and techniques that will assist you in becoming a high performer. Here I will only provide you an overview of the general approach and the value this information can provide you.

Biases

We all have biases. It is part of the heuristic which allows us to make quick determinations without investing the time and energy required to think carefully about every situation.[35] In short, we have developed shortcuts to true thinking to help us navigate our daily life more efficiently. In most cases these serve us well and are helpful. However, there are times when a bias can negatively impact our

---

[35] Blount, J. (2018, Jun. 13). *Objections: The Ultimate Guide for Mastering the Art and Science of Getting Past No*. Wiley.

thinking or our behavior. The first step to dealing with bias is to understand they exist and to become self-aware. By the way, our prospects and clients have biases as well. Understanding these will allow us to better navigate each interaction we have with them and to overcome any bias which may impede our ability to develop a mutually-beneficial relationship with them.

Listed below are a few common biases that you should be aware of to recognize them in your prospects, clients, and yourself.

Fundamental Attribution Error

This is a tendency for people to place an undue emphasis on internal characteristics (personality) to explain someone else's behavior in each situation rather than considering the situation or external factors.[36]

---

[36] McLeod, S. (2018). *Fundamental Attribution Error.* Simply Psychology. Retrieved from https://www.simplypsychology.org/fundamental-attribution.html

Self-Serving Bias

A tendency to strengthen a person's ego by attributing positive events to his own ability and attributing negative events to forces outside his control.[37] In other words, if something good happens, I did it. If something bad happens, it is bad luck or someone else's fault.

Self-Enhancement Bias

The tendency for individuals to take all the credit for their success while giving little or no credit to other individuals or external forces.[38]

---

[37] Ruhl, C. (2021, Apr. 19). *Self-Serving Bias: Definition and Examples.* Simply Psychology. Retrieved from
https://www.simplypsychology.org/self-serving-bias.html
[38] Popova, M. (n.d.). *How Our Delusions Keep Us Sane: The Psychology of Our Essential Self-Enhancement Bias.* The Marginalian. Retrieved Jan. 26, 2022, from
https://www.themarginalian.org/2014/06/04/david-mcraney-self-enchancement-bias/

Optimism Bias

When a person believes they are at a lesser risk of experiencing a negative event.[39] An inability to recognize potential risk or hazards.

Overconfidence Bias

A person's subjective confidence in his judgement is reliably greater than the objective accuracy of those judgements.[40] Simply stated, thinking I am infallible.

False Consensus and Confirmation Biases

False consensus is when a person tends to overestimate the extent to which his opinions, beliefs, preferences, values, and habits are normal and typical of others. That others think as I do.[41]

---

[39] Cherry, K. (2020, May 10). *Understanding the Optimism Bias: AKA the Illusion of Invulnerability*. Very Well Mind. Retrieved from https://www.verywellmind.com/what-is-the-optimism-bias-2795031
[40] Moore, D.A. (2018, Jan. 18). *Overconfidence: The Mother of All Biases. Psychology Today*. Retrieved from https://www.psychologytoday.com/ca/blog/perfectly-confident/201801/overconfidence
[41] Cherry, K. (2020, May 12). *How False Consensus Effect Influences the Way We Think About Others*. Very Well Mind. Retrieved from https://www.verywellmind.com/what-is-the-false-consensus-effect-2795030

Confirmation bias is when we pay attention to the information that confirms our beliefs and avoid those that are contrary.[42]

Sunk Cost Fallacy

When an individual continues a behavior or endeavor as a result of previous investment of resources (time, money, effort).[43] They continue to pursue a course of action because of the previous investment even though the current course is not going to benefit them after all, unable to quit and try something else.

The Importance of Likeability

When it comes to making a significant purchase, you will find the buyer's perception of you critically important. In most cases the buyer needs to like you to buy from you. Now, I know what you might be thinking, I'm likeable! Of course, you are. We all believe that we are likeable, and for

---

[42] Cherry, K. (2021, Jul. 30). *How Confirmation Bias Works*. Very Well Mind. Retrieved from https://www.verywellmind.com/what-is-a-confirmation-bias-2795024

the most part, this is true. However, there are ways in which you can increase your likeability and improve your ability to develop a mutually-beneficial relationship. Here are some questions that every buyer considers when they are making an investment:[44]

1. Do I like you?
2. Do you listen to me?
3. Do you make me feel important?
4. Do you understand me and my problems?
5. Do I trust and believe you?
6. Do we share the same values?
7. Do I feel that you have my best interest in mind?
8. Would I recommend you to a friend or colleague?
9. Are you reliable and consistent?
10. Would I do business with you if the roles were reversed?

---

[44] Blount, J. (2017, Mar. 20). *Sales EQ: How Ultra High Performers Leverage Sales-Specific Emotional Intelligence to Close the Complex Deal*. Wiley. p. 163.

You should think about these questions in every engagement and make sure you can honestly answer, on the prospect's behalf, 'yes' to each. Remember, how you interact with the prospect or client will drive their response to each question. Each little thing you do, or don't do, will contribute to generating either 'yes' or 'no' answer for each question. Again, people are emotional more than they are rational. You must motivate them to have a positive emotional response to you, and this is accomplished by what you say, how you say it, and what you do (your behavior during each interaction). You are either pulling them closer or pushing them away. Be sure to pull them closer.

Again, this chapter is intended to be an overview of the importance of the psychology of selling and not a complete representation of the subject. Understanding and utilizing this information is essential to developing the mindset of a high-performing sales professional.

Learning Points:

1. Psychology plays a role in the selling, buying, and decision-making process. Understanding how people feel and think is critical to understanding how to help them decide to buy from you.

2. You need to consider your own biases, as well as the biases of your prospect and clients, when you are interacting with people. While biases can help simplify our life, they can also influence our actions in negative ways. It is important to be aware of our biases and ensure they do not negatively impact our perceptions, thoughts, and actions.

3. Likability is important. While we always want to be professional, it doesn't mean we cannot also be likeable. People buy from people they like. Smile and let the world know you are friendly, caring, and genuine.

"Nothing can stop the man with the right mental attitude from achieving his goal; nothing on earth can help the man with the wrong mental attitude."

W. W. Ziege

"What made you UNIQUE yesterday, makes you a COMMODITY today, and EXTINCT tomorrow, unless you ADAPT to change."

Lee B. Salz

Chapter 15: The Importance of Differentiation

If you unable to differentiate yourself, your company, and your product or service from the competition, you are leaving your prospect no choice but to let price be the determining factor. If you are the low-cost provider, this may not be the worst thing to happen. However, there can only be one low-cost provider for a specific product or service in a market. And if you are not that person, you better learn the art of differentiation. While I will share some initial thoughts with you on this subject, you should know there are other authors who have dedicated entire books to this concept. I highly encourage you to read *Sales Differentiation* and *Sell Different!* by Lee B. Salz. He is one of the most prolific experts and authors on the subject and much of what I now know about differentiation has been influenced by his work.

When I was just starting off in B2B sales, I went to work for a company selling office copiers. I worked for the original equipment manufacturer and was assigned a sales territory. I learned a great deal from this experience, and I quickly learned the importance of differentiation. Our biggest competitor was the 'king of the hill', the premier brand. However, I did not work for them. I worked for another company that sold good products which, unfortunately, were very similar to many other products available. As a matter of fact, I often wondered if all the other brands were manufactured in the same factory in Japan and simply spray painted a different color and affixed with a different logo on the way out the door. That is how different, or 'undifferent', the product specifications were in a side-by-side comparison.

Another factor was that the office copier, at the time, was probably the most hated piece of technology known to mankind. While it was an essential device for every business, which meant every business was a prospect, the actual machines were often unreliable, finicky, and just annoying. You would be hard pressed to find someone who liked their copier. On certain days, you might find a frustrated office worker feverishly trying to push it down a flight of steps after it shredded an original document they just spent three hours typing.

To make matters worse, I was not the only person in my assigned territory selling this precise brand of copier. There were two dealers selling the exact same equipment by the same manufacturer as the one I represented directly. So, talk about competition. First, I had to convince someone to give me a shot instead of just running out and buying the premier brand. Then, I had to compete against a whole bunch of other manufacturers selling nearly identical products. And if I made it that far, I had to convince the prospect not to call one of the two local dealers who could always sell them the EXACT same device I was proposing for less money. Talk about running the gauntlet. I had to navigate various levels of competition just to get a chance of winning the business only to lose out to my own product sold through a different channel. I can assure you that this was never mentioned in the original job description.

Even then, if the prospect decided to buy the exact model I recommended but placed the order through the local dealer instead of with me, the dealer would win and my company would win, but I would lose. We were banned from matching the dealer's price or ever saying anything disparaging about them (not that I would recommend that tactic anyway). However, there was nothing preventing the dealers from questioning our service capabilities or offering steep discounts to win the business. It was far more difficult than I first imagined. However, it taught me about professional selling and, more importantly, about myself.

Here is the first rule of differentiation – YOU![45] You are what is different from what anyone else is offering. No other company has you working for them. You are unique,

---

[45] Blount, J. (2010, Jun. 21). *People Buy You: The Real Secret to What Matters Most in Business*. Wiley.

and unless you have an identical twin, there is only one of you. And this is your most important asset in the highly competitive world of sales. The sales I did succeed in making were because I helped the prospect solve a business problem and they appreciated the expertise, insights, and experience I brought to the table. They knew they could get the machine for less, but what they were rewarding was the effort I put forth to help them. By buying from me, they were acknowledging the contribution I made to the solution. You are a critical part of the product or service you sell – and never forget it.

The second rule of differentiation, as mentioned above, is when there is no apparent difference between what you are offering and the competition, you leave the prospect no choice but to use price as the determining factor.[46] If you happen to have the price advantage in every situation, you may be satisfied with this option. However, this is not the most enviable situation. You always want to be able to

---

[46] Salz, L.B. (2021, Sept. 14). Sell Different! All New Sales Differentiation Strategies to Outsmart, Outmaneuver, and Outsell the Competition. HarperCollins Leadership.

garner the greatest price point for your offering to maximize the revenue you create and the commissions you earn.[47]

Learning Points:

1. When the prospect is unable to detect a difference between what you are offering and what your competition is offering, they have no choice but to let the price determine their decision.

2. You are a key part of the difference you are selling. People must buy you as much as they are buying the product or service you are offering. Show how you are different in a way that will motivate the buyer to want to do business with you.

---

[47] Salz, L.B. (2021, Sept. 14). Sell Different! All New Sales Differentiation Strategies to Outsmart, Outmaneuver, and Outsell the Competition. HarperCollins Leadership.

"No one can ever master sales. It is a philosophy. There is always more to learn."

Lee B. Salz

"We are all storytellers. We all live in a network of stories. There isn't a stronger connection between people than storytelling."

Jimmy Neil Smith

Chapter 16: The Power of a Story

Before the written word, stories were how information was passed from one person to the next. Storytelling is a key component of our shared history, and it remains one of the most effective ways to convey information to people today. Becoming an effective storyteller is an essential skill of becoming an effective sales professional and future sales leader. People find it easier to learn from a story and often remember the details much better.[48] In this chapter, we will talk about the development and use of stories in detail.

---

[48] Boris, V. (2017, Dec. 20). Leading the Way: What Makes Storytelling So Effective For Learning? Harvard Business Publishing Corporate Learning. Retrieved from https://www.harvardbusiness.org/what-makes-storytelling-so-effective-for-learning/

Once upon a time, in a land far away, there was a new sales professional named (insert your name here), who was just beginning their journey in sales. They were enthusiastic and confident but lacked some of the critical knowledge and experience to become an effective sales professional. One day they were in the village square and heard a grey-bearded man wearing a top hat, white suit, with a red tie, selling widgets. Because he was so eccentric, they were immediately drawn in and tried to move closer to better hear and see what was going on. However, a large crowd had gathered, making it difficult to move closer. Everyone was listening intently to this interesting man with a desire to buy his magical widgets. They were stunned to see the man continue to speak as more and more people came forth with arms outstretched, holding shiny gold coins, to buy his special widgets. It was simply amazing.

Understanding that this was just a short blurb, could you see the story unfolding in your mind's eye? Did you insert yourself into the story, as the young sales professional gazing upon a bearded man in a white suite and red tie selling his widgets? Did you formulate a vision of what the man in the story looked like? The crowd pressing forward? This is the power of a story. The ability to grab your attention and pull you in. If you think about it, most stories follow a very similar pattern. The entertainment industry is notorious for exploiting a common storytelling formula in their productions. While the characters and actual story might change, the elements are nearly identical and follow a pattern that has shown to be most effective.[49]

In general, compelling stories share a few key elements which include:

- A clear purpose
- A personal connection
- Common reference points
- Detailed characters and imagery
- Conflict, vulnerability, or achievement
- A good pace (beginning, middle, and end)[50]

---

[49] Hedges, K. (2020, Oct. 20). *The Inspiration Code: How the Best Leaders Energize People Every Day*. AMACOM.
[50] Hedges, K. (2020, Oct. 20). *The Inspiration Code: How the Best Leaders Energize People Every Day*. AMACOM.

As a high-performing sales professional, I would encourage you to develop a repertoire of appropriate stories to have ready when needed. When you are new, it may be difficult to find stories in which you have been directly involved. That is fine. You can use stories from other sales professionals on your team as a basis for developing your own story library. Instead of saying, "I have a client who..." you can say something like, "My associate worked with a client in a very similar situation, and we were able to help provide a solution that exceeded their expectations." The client is interested in solving their problem or gaining an advantage, and a compelling story can help them better understand how you and your company can help them achieve those goals.

It is a good idea to create a 'story book' to capture the important details of both your successes and your company's successes in helping people. While I do not recommend giving this book to a prospect, the value is in helping you organize the various stories you may want to share. Depending on your business, you will want to have a story for each of the products or services you offer. Also consider the types of clients you have assisted. For example, perhaps you specialize in three or four vertical markets (healthcare, legal, or finance). It would be more powerful to have a story for each product or service for each of your target markets. This will help you convey the most appropriate story for maximum impact. The more specific you can be about the initial situation (the problem) and how that problem was impacting the client's business (the business implication), the more powerful your explanation of how your company was able to help them (the solution or need pay-off). Remember, if all you have is a hammer, everything will look like a nail. Broaden your toolbox to be prepared to handle all manner of screws, bolts, and fasteners.

Learning Points:

1. Stories are inherent to how humans communicate information and learn. If done well, it is a powerful way to engage the prospect and convey critical information in order to highlight key points that will help you sell more effectively.

2. A great story draws the prospect into the story. They can see themselves as the center of the story. It will help your prospect visualize the process of moving from the initial problem and the impact it is having on their business, to realizing the benefits of taking action to resolve these issues by collaborating with you.

3. Consider compiling a story book with the key facts of clients you or your company have helped. This way you can share a story related to a shared industry or challenge to increase the relevance for the prospect. Create a diverse toolbox to have the right tool for each situation. Visit www.practical-sales-wisdom.com for detailed instructions on how to build your own story book.

"Great storytelling can make the difference between someone paying attention to you and someone just tuning you out."

Christopher S. Penn

Section 4: Next Steps

"An investment in knowledge pays the best interest."
Benjamin Franklin

Chapter 17: Financial Considerations

Here is some advice on the financial considerations you need to know as a sales professional. While some of these items will appear quite intuitive, I would encourage you to take the time to ensure you understand how each works for the company you represent. Every company is different, and assumptions may lead you to disappointment. It amazes me how often a salesperson is unaware of exactly how their compensation plan is structured or how to leverage it for maximum personal gain. Clearly understand all the financial implications of your position so you can position yourself to earn what you deserve.

Compensation Plans

It is critically important for you to clearly understand your compensation plan to maximize your earnings and achieve the performance level stipulated by your company. These plans come in a wide variety with various components. However, all compensation plans share one thing in common – they direct behavior. It is important to review your plan to understand what results the company values most and how you can focus to achieve these results to maximize your earnings.

Since compensation plans vary significantly from company to company, it would be unreasonable to try and describe every possible plan. What I will attempt to do is bring to your attention some of the key components often found in compensation plans and to make you aware of their potential impact on you. It will be incumbent on you to carefully read and review your plan and see which of these concepts applies to your situation. If after reviewing, you have questions about your compensation plan you should arrange a meeting with your manager to review the contents and to ensure there are no misunderstandings about how the plan works or how your results will be compensated.

Commissions

Companies have various ways for compensating sales professionals for actual revenue generated. Again, you want to be crystal clear on how you will earn commissions. In some cases, you will be paid a percentage based on the actual revenue generated. Some plans have 'escalators' that increase the percentage payout as you reach different levels of revenue. The more you sell, the more you earn.

Some companies compensate sales professionals on the gross profit of each transaction. Instead of being rewarded purely on the revenue they will compensate you on the gross profit which measures the profitability of the revenue you generated. If you are selling at higher prices, the gross profit will be better, and you will earn a higher commission as a result. Depending on the industry, and competitive factors, the desire to charge a premium price should be balanced with the ability to win the business. In other words, you may want to sell at the list price every time, but this approach might jeopardize the amount of business you can win. While I am not advocating for selling at the minimum level, you need to understand the correlation between the pricing levels, your win rate, and eventually your earnings.

You should also understand if there are deductions or reductions for specific issues. For example, some companies have a charge back for commissions if a client fails to pay their invoice upon being issued credit terms. Or others may reduce the commission payout if you sell below the minimum price point. Again, these rules vary, but it is your job to know how they might impact you and what you can do to mitigate any deductions.

You should review your commission statements and payments when they are issued. Never assume you are being properly paid. Having worked for both small and large companies, I can tell you firsthand that errors have been made. Please do not confuse this with intentionality or acts of malice. It is simply that many plans require human intervention in calculating the payments, and people make mistakes. If you make it a regular habit of checking your statements, you can alert your manager when an item needs to be reviewed or adjusted. You earned it, so make sure you receive it.

Bonuses and Special Incentives

Does your compensation plan offer a bonus in addition to commissions? Bonus plans may be monthly, quarterly, or annually to provide extra incentive to exceed your sales target. For example, your plan may state that for each quarter you achieve 110% of your quarterly sales quota you will be paid a bonus which is either a flat amount or some percentage of the revenue or gross profit you generated. Some plans are based on your annual performance. In either case, you will want to understand the bonus structure so you can manage your opportunities accordingly. For example, if you are coming to the end of the quarter and you are on the cusp of reaching your bonus, it might make sense to lower the price on a particular transaction to attain your bonus. The commission you sacrificed on that one deal may be well offset by the bonus you will earn. Again, every plan is different, which is why it is so important for you to understand the incentives and payment structure.

Some companies also offer trips or special events to reward their top performers. They often have specific guidelines for achieving the recognition and the reward. Be sure to understand all the rules governing these special bonuses. They are generally based on your annual performance results but may have other stipulations which require selling a certain number of units, or specific ancillary services, or achieving a specific activity level. Since they are all different be sure to understand what is required to earn the distinction of a top performer.

Gates and Special Requirements

Your compensation plan may have gates or other special requirements that you must fulfill to earn the maximum commission on each transaction or to be eligible for a bonus. For example, you may work for a company that sells multiple products, but there is a requirement that you sell a minimum of two specific items every month. If you do so, you will earn an additional percentage on all the revenue you generate during the month. Companies often do this to drive sales of a highly-profitable item with sluggish sales or when they want to redirect the efforts of the sales organization to sell a new product or service. Remember, compensation plans are about driving specific behaviors. In this case, your company wants you to sell more of this item and, in return for earning a commission for selling it, they will also pay you even more on everything else you sold that month. In some cases, the gate is an annual target which will impact all the revenue or gross profit you generated for the year.

Gates are an interesting topic. While it makes sense for the company to want to focus your attention on a particular set of products or services, there may be reasons why the sales organization is not selling these items. I remember a case when I worked for a company that sold office equipment. I managed a senior team with a large quota and the company put in a gate to sell two printers each quarter. In the scheme of things, these devices were a mere fraction of the price of the products we typically sold. Even if you did manage sell two of these devices per quarter, the total revenue generated would be negligible.

My team was not happy with this requirement. If they failed to sell two printers each quarter, they would not be eligible for their quarterly bonus. Remember, I said compensation plans are designed to motivate certain behaviors. My team lamented they did not have the time to sell such an inconsequential product. It was not worth the effort, except that their bonus depended upon achieving this requirement.

Once they were done complaining about the situation, I acknowledged the difficulty we faced in selling them and suggested we simply give the printers away. Well, not exactly give them away for free, but include them in our recommendations as an added benefit to our clients. Essentially, we would adjust the pricing on the larger transactions and tell the client we were including a new printer as a part of a special promotion. This was an easy solution to the problem, and it would make both the sales professionals and company happy. My team had no trouble giving away the printers, often using it to differentiate our overall offering and value. This allowed them to win more business as well as earn their quarterly bonuses.

If you review your compensation plan and discover a similar requirement you can certainly spend time focused to selling the specific product or service to reach the gate requirement. However, you may want to consider using your creativity to find an easier way to achieve the goal and to maximize your earnings. While you are expected to work hard it does not mean the work itself has to be difficult. A simple change of perspective is often enough to find a better way to achieve the same or better result.

There is another reason it is important to clearly understand your compensation plan before you accept a position or when a new plan is released to the salesforce. You need to know what is expected and how you can best leverage the plan to earn the maximum income potential amount offered. On that point, compensation plans should be leveraged. You have the right, and obligation, to understand what the company wants and how they will compensate you for a certain behavior (result). Then, you need to figure out how you can take advantage of the plan to earn the most money on the sales and revenue you generate. I have seen many times how a sales professional who really understood their compensation plan was able to earn substantially more money than a co-worker who generated more revenue. Not all plans are created equally, and revenue generation alone does not ensure the maximum payout. Compensation plans are designed to motivate behavior. Understand what your company wants most and find a way to maximize your results accordingly.

General Items

Most compensation plans offer an annual salary paid on a regular basis. You may also be eligible for certain stipends. This may include a car allowance if you use your vehicle for business purposes. Be sure you know if you will be paid a flat stipend or if you are required to report business mileage. If you must report your mileage, be sure to understand what if any documentation is required. You may have to report your actual mileage for each business day or just the monthly total. Create an appropriate system to track this activity to ensure you are properly reimbursed when you submit your expense report. Some companies also provide a technology allowance for cell phone and internet usage. Essentially, they are asking you to use your own devices and then are offering you reimbursement for the time you use these items for work.

Expense Reimbursement

You will also want to understand if your company offers an expense reimbursement plan for business expenses while performing your duties. This could include reimbursement for parking, tolls, a client or networking partner meal, or attending professional events. Generally, if the company allows for these expenses, you will likely have to submit a report with receipts. Be sure you ask if there are limitations either per event or per month. Some companies will reimburse any reasonable business expense. Others may set a dollar limit for meals or events. If you plan to spend more, you may be required to secure approval in advance. If you want to be reimbursed for your business expenses, be sure you understand your company's policies and procedures to avoid any conflicts.

Learning Points:

1. Understand how you will be compensated and leverage the plan to maximize your earning potential. Where does the company want you to focus your attention? What incentives have they provided for you to focus on certain products or services?

2. How can you maximize your earnings? What activities will lead to the results most prized by your organization and provide you the greatest financial rewards? Each company has a business objective and will typically reward sales professionals at a higher rate when their activities and results are aligned with these overall goals.

3. Reimbursement for typical business expenses is common. To ensure you can be reimbursed for all

legitimate expenses, understand the policies governing spending and be sure to understand how and when to submit expense reports.

"Guess a thing ain't knowing a thing."

Patrick Ness

"Don't deliver a product. Deliver an experience."

Unknown

Chapter 18: Develop a Support Team

Most sales professionals do not have a dedicated resource, like an assistant, assigned to them. While this is unfortunate, since it would certainly improve the productivity of even elite performers, it is a reality. As a result, some salespeople erroneously think they must do everything themselves. This is limited thinking in a world of infinite possibilities.[51] It is your responsibility to work as efficiently as possible. The way to really 'multiply' your efforts is to have a team working with you, to make it easier to focus on the things only you can do, while providing your prospects and clients a great overall experience. Today clients and prospects are buying an experience as much as they are buying a specific product or service. You need to make working with you a positive, memorable experience

---

[51] Sinek, S. (2019, Oct. 15). *The Infinite Game*. Portfolio.

to differentiate yourself from your competitors and from every other sales professional trying to get their attention.

You probably have the basis of an effective team right now, but because they don't directly report to you, or have a title that says, "Assistant to Sales Professional," you may not recognize them for what they could be. I say "could be" because developing a support team takes some work. However, if done correctly, this investment will pay for itself every day of the week and twice on Sunday.

What type of support team do I need?

This is the starting point. It will vary to some degree based on your company, but we will focus on a typical situation. A support team is another one of those things readily available to each sales professional in your office, but only the top 10% will ever leverage these resources to maximize their efforts. You should start by thinking about the people you met with in Chapter 7. Here you sought out the best of the best to learn what they do and how it can impact you and your clients. Are you able to solicit these people to be a part of your team?

The key to success in this area is to recognize you are dealing with people. People, who just like you, act in their own best self-interest. They have a job and responsibilities, and they are not going to drop what they are doing to satisfy you when you snap your fingers. Unless, of course, they view doing so as furthering their own self-interest. Just like building any other type of mutually-beneficial relationship, you are going to have to invest the time and effort to get other people to want to help you. You need to forge productive work friendships so you can accomplish more in less time.

In many organizations there is a traditional tug-of-war between the sales organization and almost every other department. It really comes down to the way we, sales professionals, think and behave. Most sales professionals are highly creative thinkers who excel at solving problems. Most of the other people in your organization are analytical and follow processes, procedures, and rules. And, as we already know, sales professionals, for the most part, have never met a rule they wouldn't stretch, break, avoid, or otherwise ignore. This is, in my humble opinion, the systemic root of the problem and the source of the friction which can exist in some organizations. However, if you are smart, it can also be a way to differentiate yourself from the rest and become the best. You can earn a reputation as someone who is not "a typical salesperson" and get better assistance and support from the entire team.

The way for you to overcome this challenge is to treat the various people in your office like you would a prospect or client. You need to develop a relationship, so they like you. Plain and simple. Let me ask you this, if a good friend asked you for a favor, would you do it? Absolutely. If a colleague you despised ask you for the same favor, would you do it? Probably not. It really is not complicated. The challenge is to get the people you work with to see you as a friend so they will be motivated to help you. And that begins with you. Yes, you will have to do the lion's share of the work.

But, in the end, you will be the one to benefit the most. It will be well worth the effort.

Everyone wants to be liked. Life is much more fun that way. Each of us needs to increase our likeability. To do that, we must behave in a way that benefits the other person. Sure, there are things about your personality that may increase your attractiveness, but, in the end, you must think in terms of the other person and respect their likes and dislikes. For example, you may have a sales support administrator who is not a morning person. Do yourself a favor and stop calling her when she first arrives at work, making demands on her time. Is it that hard to see that she is not ready to greet the world with a smile until after her second cup of Joe? These small acts of acknowledgement will show you care, and the people you work with will be much more willing to support you by doing the little extras to make your life easier.

Set Clear Expectations

As you develop your support team it is important to realize you will need to 'manage' them as if they were reporting to you. Please do not confuse 'manage' with bossing them around. We have already discussed the special nature of this relationship. You do not have power over them, but you can cultivate a degree of influence. As you begin to work together, be sure to thank them for their efforts. An expression of gratitude goes a long way. Remember, you want to establish yourself as different so you will receive better support.

You will also want to set certain expectations for the support provided, to ensure your team accomplishes the tasks where you require assistance. It is important to give them boundaries and to share your thoughts on the outcomes you desire. This does not mean that you tell them how to do the work. Rather you share with them the results you are looking to achieve. For example, your clients may reach out to your customer service representative which in turn requires you to visit the client. You may want to share your calendar with your customer service representative so they can schedule the appointment on your behalf, saving both you and your client an additional phone call.

If you decide to proceed this way, take the time to share with your customer service representative how they should schedule a meeting on your behalf, to remain consistent with maximizing your time. Let them know that you would like them to book the appointment near another appointment in the same geographic area. You may want to share with them the technique of saying, "Yes, Sales Professional (name) will be in your area on Thursday afternoon. Might you be available at either 1:00 PM or 2:00 PM for a visit?" Never assume that someone else knows what you want to achieve. Ask for their help, explain what would be helpful, and then follow up to ensure they accomplish the desired result.

You will not gain efficiencies if your support team makes extra work for you. The goal is for them to take tasks off your plate so you can stay focused on sales activities that generate revenue and commissions. By sharing your desired outcome with them, they will know how to best support you and you will both benefit from a relationship based on effective communication and mutual understanding. It is a process that will require both time and patience to foster. However, if done correctly, will pay long-term dividends for you and your ability to grow your business.

 Visit www.practical-sales-wisdom.com to access the **My Personal Support Team Worksheet**.

Learning Points:

1. Everyone can use help to improve their efficiency and effectiveness. Developing a support team to help you do your best work each day is a great time investment.

2. Manage your team and set clear expectations. Never assume they know what you want or expect. Engage in meaningful dialogue to help them effectively help you. And always be willing to do what you can to make their life easier as well.

3. Your team will require time to establish and become a strategic resource. One of the most important things is

to demonstrate ongoing gratitude and appreciation for their assistance. Take every opportunity to thank them for being there to support you. Celebrate new clients and sales success to recognize the efforts of your team's contributions.

"There's nothing greater in the world than when somebody on the team does something good, and everybody gathers around to pat him on the back."

Billy Martin

"The difference between a successful person and others is not a lack of strength, not a lack of knowledge, but rather a lack of will."

Vince Lombardi

Chapter 19: Get Involved!

One of my favorite interview questions to ask a candidate is, "If we were to go duck hunting, what would be the most important factor in planning the trip?" Do not worry, no ducks were harmed in this example. The purpose of the question is to see if they can think about it in the simplest terms. What is most important? What do you think the best answer is? If you said to "go where the ducks are" you are correct! You may have found this question elementary, but you would be amazed at the wide array of answers I have received over the years. The most important thing about duck hunting is not the right clothing, or the equipment, or a faithful golden retriever. While all these things may offer some advantages, the **destination** is the most critical factor. If you select the desert as your destination, you will never see a duck, no matter how many times you blow on that duck call. No, the important factor is to go where the ducks are. More than anything else this simple truth will determine your level of success.

I am using this example to illustrate the importance of investing your networking and business development activities in the most productive manner. There is nothing worse in terms of time or personal sanity than calling on the wrong prospects. While you will feel busy, you will not be productive or effective. You will become frustrated from the lack of success, despite the effort, if you do not spend your time with the right prospects. Quite frankly, you are chasing a particular type of duck, known to many as the ideal prospect. These people tend to congregate in common areas. You know the adage, birds of a feather flock together (ok, enough with the bird analogies). Your clients and prospects will typically join and participate in certain organizations, trade associations, and other professional networking groups with other professionals like themselves. It is essential for you to understand where they spend their time, either in person, or now, virtually, so you can invest your time there as well. It is one of the best methods for identifying and securing new clients as well as to be seen as an involved member of the community. People respond to people who are like themselves. Become one of them. Invest your time with the greatest opportunity for a positive return on investment.

In Chapter 7, we reviewed questions you can ask existing clients to learn more about why they chose to work with your firm. This is also an excellent time to ask your point of contact about groups or trade associations to which they belong. If the client you have is an ideal client, then you can learn about where they spend their time and where you are likely to find other people with similar needs. Your company may already belong to specific organizations to promote their offerings. It is important to research these groups and select the ones that provide you the best opportunity for strategic introductions and meaningful interactions.

While many of these organizations have a social component, such as hosting 'happy hours', you should focus on productive uses of your time. There is nothing wrong with attending parties or golf outings. You will certainly meet some people and make some new connections. However, every sales professional from across every known industry will also be attending these same outings, so your efforts may be diluted. Rather than being just like everyone else, commit to standing out by becoming an active member whenever possible. One of the best ways to do this is by volunteering to be a member of a committee. You may even join the committee that plans and hosts the social events. In doing so, you will show a greater commitment to the success of the organization than those salespeople who just show up for the parties. While this does involve some additional effort on your part, I think you will find the benefits are quickly realized.

You can also build relationships with other volunteers, the 'movers and shakers'. If these people are donating their time to the organization, you know they are invested. It is important to them. And your desire to be a part of it will set you apart from other sales professionals. You may also find these people will be willing to make introductions to other members, noting that you are on their committee and providing support to the organization. You will be a part of the inside crowd while other salespeople are on the outside looking in.

There may be times when vendors are not allowed to participate on a committee. Do not let this deter your interest in joining or participating. Consider contacting the organization's president and asking if there is some other way you could assist. Most organizations are happy to get assistance because there is always more work to do than time allows. Plus, you will make a connection with the leader of the organization who is likely the best person to make strategic introductions so you can quickly integrate yourself into the group.

For example, you could offer to come to the meetings early to help set up and distribute the name tags. This is a simple way to meet nearly everyone who will attend the meeting.

Think about the benefits of getting to say hello to every member each month as they come through the door. Your presence and willingness to assist will impress them, and you will become a known entity in no time at all. Familiarity breeds trust and trust opens the door to developing mutually-beneficial relationships. You will find that these members are much more willing to meet with you once they begin to see you on a regular basis. Once they see you as a member of their club, you are no longer a 'salesperson' but our new member and friend, Vince.

Another critical advantage to joining these groups is the ability to meet and network with other high-performing sales professionals like yourself. These contacts will be a great source of information about the group and profession in general. Further, you may want to start a 'leads' group to share information and make business introductions for each other. As we know, a warm introduction beats a cold call any day.

Virtual Networking Communities

While most of this chapter was dedicated to live interaction, we should recognize the growing presence of virtual communities. You should become aware of and participate in these online groups as well. The easiest way to start is to search for relevant groups on a professional social media platform, like LinkedIn. Often there are groups which allow anyone to participate, while others require the host to permit you to join. Evaluate each for relevancy and determine which might gain you access to important potential connections as well as important industry insights. Learn who the thought leaders are - they are the ones posting key information and have a significant number of followers. Note what topics appear to be 'hot' in your industry right now. Join in the discussion where you can add value. Don't be a commercial for your company. Don't focus on selling a product or service. Contribute meaningful insights you have gleaned over time in your role so you can become a thought leader as well.

You may also discover other online communities or user groups by searching the internet. Depending on your industry, you may find the online community more vibrant than the in-person community. Again, here is an opportunity to learn more about your industry and make new connections. While I prefer face-to-face networking opportunities, the world is rapidly changing and there are many virtual networking groups with new ones popping up all the time. Virtual groups have the benefit of allowing you to contribute during non-selling hours and find connections all over the world. Many of the basic premises still apply to the virtual world. You need to actively participate in the discussions, share thoughtful information, and work to become a recognized member of that community through your consistent efforts. Nothing worth doing is easy. Invest the time to become a recognized, contributing member of these groups. Take advantage of every opportunity to build a strong network and develop mutually-beneficial relationships.

 Visit www.practical-sales-wisdom.com to access **The Get Involved Planner**.

Learning Points:

1. People like people who are similar to themselves. You want to be seen as a member of their community by participating in events and groups in which they are involved.

2. Networking groups, associations, and trade organizations are a great way to connect with your target audience and your ideal prospects. It will provide you time to meet new people, develop connections, and eventually engage them in a sales opportunity. Be sure to become an active participant and regularly attend events to show your commitment.

3. Even if you are unable to join a particular group or be involved in a committee, there are other ways to get involved. Ask about sponsorships. These are opportunities to attend a meeting because you are making a financial donation to the event. Often groups will even provide you few moments to introduce yourself and talk about the problems your business can solve for them.

4. Remember to investigate virtual communities in your industry. You can join these groups to follow key members, comment on relevant topics, and provide thoughtful information, becoming a recognized contributor and thought leader. This will enhance your personal brand and attract others to follow or contact you as well.

"For myself I am an optimist – it does not seem to be much use being anything else."

Winston Churchill

"If you're not making mistakes, then you're not doing anything. I'm positive that a doer makes mistakes."

John Wooden

Chapter 20: Conclusion

I hope you have found this book useful. More importantly, I hope you actually use this book to improve yourself and the results you achieve. It was designed to be a resource guide to help you jump start your sales career and become a high-performing sales professional. While reading it is a start, your ability to implement the concepts, ideas, and suggestions is what will distinguish you as one of the best and not just part of the rest.

I like the John Wooden quote at the start of this chapter. We often find we are hesitant to try new things because we are afraid to fail. There is nothing greater than the opportunity to fail, for it is the only way for us to learn, develop, mature, and become the best version of ourselves. The people who are 'stuck' in this world are the ones who are afraid of putting forth the necessary effort to try and improve their situation. They are afraid of taking a risk. And in many cases, they are afraid of the uncertainty that comes from change. I have read we are motivated more by the desire to avoid pain than we are to seek pleasure. In other words, even if we think we might be able to improve our situation, we might not be able to overcome the risk of potential discomfort or pain to get to a better place. How unfortunate. It is only when we stretch ourselves, we begin to realize what we are truly capable of achieving. Reading this book is a good first step in improving your situation and determining your future success. I encourage you to try these techniques with the understanding they may not always work as intended. Do not despair, try again. These techniques have been developed over a lifetime of professional selling. Trust me when I first started, success did not come easily. It was grit, a combination of determination and perseverance, which made the difference.[52] And I am confident grit will make the difference for you as well.

---

[52] Duckworth, A. (2016, May 3). *Grit: The Power of Passion and Perseverance*. Collins.

You can also contact me directly to pose a question or request some additional information. While I cannot promise to have every answer, I am certainly willing to assist you when possible. I would appreciate the opportunity to learn what is on your mind. Contact me at practicalsaleswisdom@gmail.com.

The next section contains a reprint of many of the questions posed in example reviewed. I encourage you to use these questions, as well as developing your own questions to use. Questions, to me, are the most powerful tool we have, not just as sales professionals but as people, to learn and understand. Take the time to ask thoughtful questions and always follow up with additional questions to probe and discover the true underlying information and motivations of the person with which you are conversing. You will be amazed at the difference in your interactions once you have mastered this critical life skill.

Please be sure to review the Recommended Reading list at the end of the book. I have read more than 300 books on sales, sales management, leadership, and psychology. There is always something new to learn. I have listed for you some of my favorite authors and titles. They are worthy of your time if you want to continue your journey to become a high-performing sales professional. You may find that obtaining some of these books in audio format will help you to leverage your time while traveling in the car.

 Please remember to visit www.practical-sales-wisdom.com to access all the free content referred to in this book, including the **Jumpstart Your Career In Sales Checklist.** There are many documents that will help you be even more successful. Check back from time to time for new information and resources!

You may also want to consider my first book entitled *A Daily Dose of Sales Wisdom* as another resource. It is filled with 365 helpful hints, techniques, quotes, learning points, and questions you can put to work immediately to become an ultra-high performer. It also has recommendations on sales management and leadership.

Remember, be wary of anyone who claims to have the secret to sales success. There is rarely only one correct way which will work for everyone. Instead, become a student of our profession and learn something daily. Make learning a part of your professional development and be sure to access information from various sources before you commit to any one philosophy. There is an extensive amount of great information available if you just take the time to look for it.

Wishing you success in your professional sales journey!

Vince

"Don't celebrate closing a sale, celebrate opening a relationship."

Patricia Fripp

Acknowledgements

I would like to take this opportunity to thank James "Jim" Stevens for his contributions to this book. Jim and I worked together at JK Moving Services for several years before he decided to move to Phoenix to start the Commercial Moving Division of Muscular Men Moving. Jim is an ultra-high-performing sales professional, and now, a great sales leader. When I refer to the top 10% of sales professionals in this book, you can place Jim in the top 1% of this elite group. He models the way for top sales performance. I am proud of him and look forward to his continued growth as a sales and business leader. Thank you, Jim, for taking the time to lend your expertise to the writing and editing of this publication. Your insights are greatly appreciated.

I would like to thank John Asher of Asher Strategies for providing me some great information about the current sales environment and recent changes to the profession of sales. John is a prolific author and powerful speaker with a consulting practice, which has successfully trained thousands of sales professionals to become elite performers. I learn something new each time I have the pleasure to speak with him. I highly recommend his books and consultation.

And thank you to my youngest brother, Domenick Burruano, who recently embarked on a new career in sales. He was instrumental in reading this book and providing feedback from the very perspective it was designed to help – someone new to sales. His insights and suggestions were extremely valuable in completing this work. Thanks Bud!

About the Author

Vincent D. Burruano received his MBA in Business Administration, Management and Operations from The George Washington University and his Bachelor of Philosophy from the School of Philosophy at the Catholic University of America, both located in Washington, DC. Vincent has also received the following certifications: Top-Ten Sales Skills of Elite Salespeople (ASHER Global Leaders in Growth Strategies), Predictive Index (PI Worldwide), and SPIN Selling and Managing the Complex Sale (Huthwaite International). Vincent has extensive experience recruiting, coaching, developing, and leading sales professionals, selling products and services across multiple industries in several US markets. He was most recently Vice President of Sales for the Commercial Division of JK Moving Services, one of the nation's largest independent movers, in Sterling, Virginia. Today, he operates his own consulting business, Vince Burruano Consulting Services, LLC in Mount Pleasant, South Carolina.

Vincent has experience in challenging, and changing, paradigms to achieve improved results. As a leader, he promotes a culture that values trust, respect, and collaboration, in order to foster continuous improvement. Vincent is passionate about working with people who want to succeed, and who find purpose in helping their clients, co-workers, and business partners achieve their goals. He believes learning and growth are the key to success at both the individual and team levels. Vincent practices a customer-centric approach that encourages mutually-beneficial relationships.

In his spare time, Vincent is an avid reader and enjoys traveling. He has been a volunteer first responder and firefighter, a football and baseball coach, served on the Board of Directors and Executive Sales Leadership Team with the Office Moving Alliance, and is a Member of the Lido Civic Club of Washington, DC. Vincent also serves as a Forbes Business Development Council Member, writing articles for their members. Vincent has recently written his first book, *A Daily Dose of Sales Wisdom: Practical Advice for Sales Professionals and Leaders to Excel.*

Specialties include Building and Leading High-Performance Teams, New Business Development, Driving Organic Growth, Enterprise Sales Strategy, Sales Process Improvement, Individual Professional Development Planning, Change Management, Collaboration, Project Management, CRM Implementation and Utilization, and Performance Management.

You are invited to contact the author at practicalsaleswisdom@gmail.com to ask questions or share ideas. You are also welcomed to connect via LinkedIn at www.linkedin.com/in/vincent-burruano.

Website: www.practical-sales-wisdom.com

Appendix 1: The Power of Questions Review

This section captures many of the questions presented in the earlier chapters of the book. They have been reprinted here for quick reference. I encourage you to develop you own list of questions to complement what is here so you will be properly prepared for each opportunity. Remember, whoever is asking the questions is the person driving the conversation. Let the prospect provide you the information you the knowledge you need to win the business and develop mutually-beneficial relationships.

Chapter 5

I appreciate your willingness to meet with me. I will be near your office this coming Thursday. Would you be available to see me at 9:30 AM or would 1:00 PM be more convenient?

Chapter 7

I was wondering if you could help me. I am new to XYZ Company and the industry in general, I was hoping you might be willing to share some of your experiences as a way for me to learn more about the business?

Questions to ask when you are interviewing a current client:

Why do you do business with my company?

What do we do well? Where could we improve?

Who did you do business with before us? What, if anything, prompted you to switch providers?

How did you decide to select our company? What is the process your company uses to make these types of decisions?

What organizations do you belong to? How do you keep current on industry trends?

What are your priorities for the balance of the year? Is there anything I can do to be of assistance to you?

Questions to ask a prospect about their current vendor:

Why do you do business with your current supplier?

What do they do well? Is there anything they could do differently?

Who did you do business with before them? What, if anything, prompted you to switch providers?

How did you decide to select this company? What is the process your company uses for making these types of decisions?

What organizations do you belong to? How do you keep current on industry trends?

What are your priorities for the balance of the year? Is there anything I can do to be of assistance to you?

Chapter 9

So that I am properly prepared for our meeting, could you please provide me a quick overview of your (project/need/issue/problem)?

Has anything changed since we last spoke?

I really appreciate your business. Do you happen to know of anyone else who might benefit from our products or services?

My best new clients come from referrals from people like you. I noticed on LinkedIn you are connected to Mr. Prospect and Mrs. Prospect. Do you know them well? I was wondering if you would be willing to introduce me. They work for companies which may have a need for the services I offer. Would you be willing to help me?

Chapter 10

Would it be ok if I took some notes?

Would you mind if I review my notes with you to ensure I captured the information you provided correctly?

Chapter 11

"Is there anything else we could do or offer that would make what I just explained even better?"

Appendix 2: Recommended Reading List

Anderson, S., & Stein, D. (2016). *Beyond the Sales Process: 12 Proven Strategies for a Customer-Driven World* (Illustrated). AMACOM.

Asher, J. (2017). *Close Deals Faster: The 15 Shortcuts of the Asher Sales Method.* Ideapress Publishing.

Asher, J. (2022). *The Future of Sales: The 50+ Techniques, Tools, and Processes Used by Elite Salespeople.* Simple Truths.

Asher, J. (2019). *The Neuroscience of Selling: Proven Sales Secrets to Win Over the Buyer's Heart and Mind.* Simple Truths.

Bartick, G. A., & Bartick, P. (2009). *Silver Bullet Selling: Six Critical Steps to Opening More Relationships and Closing More Sales.* John Wiley & Sons.

Bennis, W. (2009). *On Becoming a Leader: The Leadership Classic* (4th Edition). Basic Books.

Blanchard, K. H., & Johnson, S. (1985). *The One Minute Manager.* Berkley Publishing Group.

Blount, J. (2015). *Fanatical Prospecting: The Ultimate Guide to Opening Sales Conversations and Filling the*

Pipeline by Leveraging Social Selling, Telephone, Email, Text, and Cold Calling (1st Edition). Wiley.

Blount, J. (2020). *INKED: The Ultimate Guide to Powerful Closing and Sales Negotiation Tactics that Unlock YES and Seal the Deal* (1st Edition). Wiley.

Blount, J. (2010). *People Buy You: The Real Secret to What Matters Most in Business* (1st Edition). Wiley.

Blount, J. (2017). *Sales EQ: How Ultra High Performers Leverage Sales-Specific Emotional Intelligence to Close the Complex Deal* (1st Edition). Wiley.

Cialdini, R. B. (2014). *Influence: Science and Practice*. Pearson.

Collins, J. (2001). *Good To Great: Why Some Companies Make the Leap...And Others Don't* (Illustrated). Harper Business.

Drucker, P. F. (2008). *The Essential Drucker: The Best of Sixty Years of Peter Drucker's Essential Writings on Management* (Reissue Edition). Harper Business.

Duckworth, A. (2016). *Grit: The Power of Passion and Perseverance.* Collins.

Ellis, T. (2022). *B.U.D. Better, Unique, & Desirable: The Sales Process That Gets Results*. Thomas Ellis.

Ferrazzi, K. (2020). *Leading Without Authority: Why You Don't Need to Be in Charge to Inspire Others and Make Change Happen*. Penguin Business.

Gitomer, J. (2004). *Little Red Book of Selling: 12.5 Principles of Sales Greatness* (Illustrated). Bard Press.

Gladwell, M. (2008). *Outliers: The Story of Success*. Back Bay Books, Little, Brown and Company.

Glazer, R. (2019). *Elevate: Push Beyond Your Limits and Unlock Success in Yourself and Others* (Illustrated). Simple Truths.

Goldfayn, A. (2020). *5-Minute Selling: The Proven, Simple System That Can Double Your Sales...Even When You Don't Have Time*. Wiley.

Goldfayn, A. (2018). *Selling Boldly: Applying the New Science of Positive Psychology to Dramatically Increase Your Confidence, Happiness, and Sales* (1st Edition). Wiley.

Gordon, J. (2017). *The Power of Positive Leadership: How and Why Positive Leaders Transform Teams and Organizations and Change the World* (1st Edition). Wiley.

Kouzes, J. M., & Posner, B. Z. (2003). *Encouraging the Heart: A Leader's Guide to Rewarding and Recognizing Others* (Illustrated). Jossey-Bass.

Kouzes, J. M., & Posner, B. Z. (2017). *The Leadership Challenge: How to Make Extraordinary Things Happen in Organizations* (6th Edition). Wiley.

Lencioni, P. (2004). *Death by Meeting: A Leadership Fable* (1st Edition). Jossey-Bass.

Lencioni, P. (2012). *The Advantage: Why Organizational Health Trumps Everything Else in Business* (1st Edition). Jossey-Bass.

Lencioni, P. (2002). *The Five Dysfunctions of a Team: A Leadership Fable*. Jossey-Bass.

Magnuson, L. D. (2019). *The TOP Sales Leader Playbook: How to Win 5X Deals Repeatedly.* Top Line Sales.

Maxwell, J. C. (2008). *Developing the Leader Within You; Developing the Leaders Around You*. T. Nelson.

Maxwell, J. C. (2020). *Leader's Greatest Return: Attracting, Developing, and Multiplying Leaders*. HarperCollins Leadership.

Nirell, L. (2014). *The Mindful Marketer: How to Stay Present and Profitable in a Data-Driven World*. Palgrave Macmillan.

Onarecker, K. (2022). *Selling Smarter: Achieve Your Quota, Get Back on Track, & Work Strategically*. Onarecker Consulting.

Pink, D. H. (2011). *Drive: The Surprising Truth About What Motivates Us* (Illustrated). Riverhead Books.

Pollard, M., & Lewis, D. (2021). *The Introvert's Edge to Networking: Work the Room. Leverage Social Media. Develop Powerful Connections.* HarperCollins Leadership.

Rackham, N. (1988). *SPIN Selling*. McGraw-Hill Education.

Salz, L. (2018). *Sales Differentiation: 19 Powerful Strategies to Win More Deals at the Prices You Want* (Illustrated). AMACOM.

Samoisette, M. (2018). *Sales Proce$$ified: How Small Business CEOs Can Implement a Sales Process That Gets Results*. Elevate Coaching Press.

Scott, K. (2019). *Radical Candor: Be a Kick-Ass Boss Without Losing Your Humanity* (Revised Edition). St. Martin's Press.

Shore, J. (2020). *Follow Up and Close the Sale: Make Easy (and Effective) Follow-up Your Winning Habit* (1st Edition). McGraw-Hill Education.

Sinek, S., Mead, D., & Docker, P. (2017). *Find Your Why: A Practical Guide for Discovering Purpose for You and Your Team* (Illustrated). Portfolio.

Sinek, S. (2009). *Start with Why: How Great Leaders Inspire Everyone to Take Action* (Illustrated). Portfolio.

Sinek, S. (2019). *The Infinite Game*. Portfolio.

Snavely, G. (2021). *Disruptive Discovery: Uncovering the Stuff That Really Matters*. Disruptive Press.

Weinberg, M. (2012). *New Sales. Simplified.: The Essential Handbook for Prospecting and New Business Development*. AMACOM.

Weinberg, M. (2016). *Sales Management. Simplified.: The Straight Truth About Getting Exceptional Results from Your Sales Team*. AMACOM.

Weinberg, M. (2019). *#SalesTruth: Debunk the Myths, Apply Powerful Principles, Win More New Sales*. HarperCollins Leadership.

Willink, J., & Babin, L. (2017). *Extreme Ownership: How U.S. Navy SEALs Lead and Win* (Illustrated). St. Martin's Press.

Wiseman, L. (2017). *Multipliers: How the Best Leaders Make Everyone Smarter* (Revised Edition, Illustrated). Harper Business.

Wooden, J., & Jamison, S. (2005). *Wooden on Leadership: How to Create a Winning Organization* (1st Edition). McGraw-Hill Education.

Yaeger, D. (2016). *Great Teams: 16 Things High-Performing Organizations Do Differently*. W Publishing Group, an imprint of Thomas Nelson.

Made in the USA
Columbia, SC
24 June 2022

61961077R10180